THE BULLY PULPIT

The

Bully Pulpit

A TEDDY ROOSEVELT BOOK OF QUOTATIONS

Edited by

H. PAUL JEFFERS

TAYLOR TRADE PUBLISHING
Lanham • New York • Oxford

Words with me are instruments. I wish to impress upon the people to whom I talk the fact that I am sincere, that I mean exactly what I say, and that I stand for things that are elemental in civilization.
—THEODORE ROOSEVELT

First Taylor Trade Publishing paperback edition 2002

This Taylor Trade Publishing paperback edition of *The Bully Pulpit* is an unabridged republication of the edition first published in Dallas, Texas in 1998, with the addition of one textual emendation. It is reprinted by arrangement with the author.

Designed by David Timmons

Published by Taylor Trade Publishing, Inc.
A Member of the Rowman & Littlefield Publishing Group
4720 Boston Way, Lanham, MD 20706

Distributed by National Book Network

A previous edition of this book was cataloged as follows by the Library of Congress:
Roosevelt, Theodore, 1858–1919
    The bully pulpit: a Teddy Roosevelt book of quotations / edited by H. Paul Jeffers.
      p.   cm.
    Includes bibliographical references.
    1. Roosevelt, Theodore, 1858–1919—Quotations. 2. Quotations, American. I. Jeffers, H. Paul (Harry Paul), 1934– II. Title.
E660.R72 1998
973.91' 1' 092– dc21   97–49388
ISBN 0-87833-149-2 (paperback)

Contents

Introduction

A hundred years ago, as Americans prepared to begin a new century, the most talked-about and quotable personality in the country was a short, reddish-haired, spectacle-wearing, robust middle-aged man named Theodore Roosevelt.

Today, as we prepare for not only a new century, but also a new millennium, our language is rich with phrases he added to it. They include "the square deal," "the lunatic fringe," "bully," "trust buster," "muckraking," "hyphenated American," "speak softly and carry a big stick," "the strenuous life," "weasel words," and a description of the White House as an address from which a president has the duty to shape public opinion: "the bully pulpit."

Historians are unanimous in describing TR as the inventor of the modern presidency, that is, an activist chief executive of a strong federal government whose chief duties are the people's welfare and a strong national defense.

As to how he was addressed (the stuffed toy bear named after him notwithstanding), no one close to him called him "Teddy." As a child he was "Teedie." As an adult he was "Theodore" or "TR."

At forty years of age (in 1898) he already had been a leader of the New York State Legislature, a candidate for mayor of New York City (defeated in 1886), a member of the

U.S. Civil Service Commission, and president of the New York Board of Police Commissioners (1895–1897).

Upon Roosevelt's appointment as assistant secretary of the navy in 1897 by President William McKinley, the Washington correspondent of the *Chicago Times-Herald* wrote that Theodore Roosevelt "is by long odds one of the most interesting of the younger men seen here in recent years."

After he was appointed to the Navy post, he used the position to almost single-handedly lead the United States into a war to kick Spain out of the Western Hemisphere and then went on to become the hero of that war as he led his cavalry unit, the Rough Riders, who fought without horses, up San Juan Hill to win a stunning victory that made Theodore Roosevelt the most famous man in all of America.

A prolific writer, he had established himself as an essayist and author of books, including *The Naval War of 1812* in 1882, *The Winning of the West*, published in four volumes between 1889 and 1896, and numerous volumes on hunting and other ways of enjoying what he called "the strenuous life." (A complete list may be found at the end of this book.) He also wrote scores of magazine articles and editorials and delivered dozens of speeches while campaigning either on behalf of himself or others. And throughout his life he turned out a prodigious amount of correspondence (one estimate placed the total at more than 150,000 pieces).

Elected governor of New York after returning in triumph from the Spanish-American War, he found himself in 1900 chosen to be vice president in William McKinley's second term. Although he had said that being vice president was akin to being a fifth wheel on a wagon, he was well on his way to fulfilling a prophecy offered by the famed and respected editor of the Emporia, Kansas, *Gazette*. William Allen White had described Roosevelt as "the new American for the Twentieth Century."

When a man with a pistol in his hand assassinated McKinley in 1901, TR moved into the presidential mansion, officially gave it the name "the White House," ordered extensive renovations to the old mansion (adding the West Wing, a tennis court, and a room for reporters), and immediately converted it into a bully pulpit on almost every issue on his public and private agendas.

Twenty years had passed since he made his debut as a speaker during his freshman year as a lawmaker in Albany when a veteran of the legislature observed that he had appeared to speak with some difficulty, "as if he had an impediment in his speech." What he had was asthma, so that his delivery was marked by moments of breathlessness that seemed to convey nervousness. Another observer of TR's first speech as an elected official noted that Roosevelt had "a wealth of mouth."

That mouth was big and wide, dominated by a set of teeth so remarkable in their appearance that they, a bushy mustache, and the nose glasses he wore for acute nearsightedness were to become hallmarks of the Roosevelt image and the perennial favorites of newspaper and magazine cartoonists. (A vivid description of TR's teeth will be found in the section "Quotations about Roosevelt.")

Historian H. G. Wells looked at him and saw a "friendly, peering snarl of a face."

Speeches by TR were also notable for their body language.

He had a lifetime habit of punctuating his remarks by pounding the fist of one hand into the palm of the other. He frequently stood with a fist clenched and jammed on a hip.

For such a short (five foot eight), stocky, and athletic young man, he had a voice that seemed inappropriately high pitched. Some of his listeners described it as raspy. But whatever might have been said about his style of delivery, no one ever accused Theodore Roosevelt of having had nothing memorable to say.

Having become president in his own right in the election of 1904, he promised every American "a square deal," gave the nation its first pure food law and the Panama Canal, carried on a vigorous campaign of "trust busting," and sent a fleet of white-painted U.S. warships on an around-the-globe cruise to show the flag and to assert that the United States was a world power to be reckoned with. After mediating peace in a war between Japan and Russia he was awarded the Nobel Peace Prize.

Two years later he was to leave his mark on the future of law enforcement in the nation by creating a staff of detectives within the Justice Department. Founded on July 16, 1908, it was assigned the task of rooting out corruption in the federal government. It was called the Bureau of Investigation and in time became the Federal Bureau of Investigation (FBI).

Out of office, restless and unhappy with his successor in the White House (President William Howard Taft), he made a bid for the Republican presidential nomination in 1912. Brushed aside by the GOP, he ran as the candidate of the new Bullmoose Party, shrugged off an assassination attempt by making a speech with a bullet in his chest, and lost the election to Woodrow Wilson.

Returning to his family (wife Edith and six children) at Sagamore Hill, Oyster Bay, New York, he wrote his autobiography and maintained a presence in public life by writing and speaking.

Always the advocate of a "strenuous life," he left his home to undertake a big-game safari in Africa that was followed by a triumphal tour of European capitals. His adventures also included exploring rugged Brazilian jungles and nearly dying while surveying an unexplored river that was promptly named Rio Teodoro in his honor.

When America entered "the Great War" in 1917 and his four sons went off to fight in it he implored President Wilson for a command but was refused. The youngest son, Quentin, an aviator, was killed when his plane was shot down in France in July 1918.

Still a potent force in politics, TR found himself being urged to make another run for the presidency in 1920. But near midnight on January 5, 1919, after writing a memorandum to the chairman of the Republican National Committee, he asked his valet to turn out a light, settled down to sleep, and never woke up. He was sixty-one years old.

As we approach not only a new century but also a new millennium, and as private and public political and social discourse speaks of a need for a return to what is termed "values," Roosevelt's wisdom and counsel before, during, and after his presidency are a wellspring of inspiration and an example for Americans today.

This volume contains examples of his wisdom and wit on subjects ranging from America and Americans to wrestling.

Also provided are Roosevelt's insights and comments on himself.

Many things he said or wrote are included simply because of their beauty and style, or because of his colorful choice of words or phrases, because there were few things that TR loved more than lively use of the American language for a moral purpose.

A separate section provides his observations, both contemporaneous and from the basis of hindsight, on his role as leader of Roosevelt's Rough Riders during the Spanish-American War and on his decisive and heroic charge up San Juan Hill, the defining moment that he called "my crowded hour."

There is also a sampling, arranged chronologically, of what others said about him throughout his career.

The high points of his life are cited in a chronology, along with the titles of his books, and for those who wish to know more about TR there is a list of books about his life and times.

Biographer John Morton Blum wrote, "The special mark of Theodore Roosevelt was joy—joy in everything he did." In *The Rise of Theodore Roosevelt*, Edmund Morris said, "No Chief Executive, certainly, has ever had so much fun. One of Roosevelt's favorite expressions is 'dee-lighted'—he uses it so often, and with such grinning emphasis, that nobody doubts his sincerity."

The makers of Maxwell House coffee didn't doubt it. Since TR told a hotel waiter he would be "dee-lighted" to have a second cup of Maxwell House because the first had been "good to the last drop," the phrase has been the coffee company's only slogan.

But, as you will find in the words of Theodore Roosevelt in this book, TR's legacy is far more than a clever line. He was and remains the measure of righteousness, publicly and privately. In the preface to his biography of TR, Nathan Miller wrote that TR "continues to cast a magic spell over the collective consciousness." In a modern world offering few genuine heroes, he went on, "Roosevelt's greatness lies in the fact that he was essentially a moral man in a world that has increasingly regarded morality as superfluous."

Quotations

AMERICA AND AMERICANS

Like all Americans, I like big things; big prairies, big forests and mountains, big wheat fields, railroads—and herds of cattle, too—big factories, steamboats, and everything else.

—Dickinson, Dakota Territory,
July 4, 1886

To bear the name of American is to bear the most honorable of titles; and whoever does not so believe has no business to bear the name at all.

—*Forum*, April 1894

We Americans have many grave problems to solve, many threatening evils to fight, and many deeds to do, if, as we hope and believe, we have the wisdom, the strength, and the courage and the virtue to do them. But we must face the facts as they are. We must neither surrender ourselves to foolish optimism, nor succumb to a timid and ignoble pessimism.

Ibid.

AMERICA AND AMERICANS
[continued]

Don't let them bluff you out of the use of the word "American." I don't [think] anything better has been done than your calling yourself the American Ambassador and using the word American instead of the United States.

> —Letter to John Hay, American ambassador to the Court of St. James in London; Washington, D.C., June 7, 1897

Is America a weakling, to shrink from the work of the great world powers? No! The young giant of the West stands on a continent and clasps the crest of an ocean in either hand. Our nation, glorious in youth and strength, looks into the future with eager eyes and rejoices as a strong man to run a race.

> Ibid.

Our country has been populated by pioneers, and therefore it has more energy, more enterprise, more expansive power than any other in the wide world.

> —Minnesota State Fair, St. Paul, September 2, 1901

The American people are slow to wrath, but when their wrath is once kindled it burns like a consuming flame.

> —First annual address to Congress, December 3, 1901

Stout of heart, we see, across the dangers, the great future that lies beyond, and we rejoice as a giant refreshed, as a strong man girt for the race; and we go down into the arena where the nations strive for mastery, our hearts lifted with the faith that to us and our children and our children's children it shall be given to make this Republic the mightiest among the peoples of mankind.

—Detroit, Michigan,
September 22, 1902

This nation is seated on a continent flanked by two great oceans. It is composed of men [who are] the descendants of pioneers, or, in a sense, pioneers themselves; of men winnowed out from among the nations of the Old World by the energy, boldness, and love of adventure found in their own eager hearts. Such a nation, so placed, will surely wrest success from fortune.

—The White House,
December 2, 1902

Ours is not the creed of the weakling and the coward; ours is the gospel of hope and triumphant endeavor.

Ibid.

The steady aim of this nation, as of all enlightened nations, should be to strive to bring nearer the day when there shall prevail throughout the world the peace of justice.

—Fourth annual message
to Congress,
December 6, 1904

AMERICA AND AMERICANS
[continued]

We are the heirs of the ages.

—Inaugural address, March 4, 1905

If we fail, the cause of free self-government throughout the world will rock to its foundations.

Ibid.

Tomorrow I shall come into office in my own right. Then watch out for me.

—The White House, March 4, 1905

I believe the majority of the plain people of the United States will, day in and day out, make fewer mistakes in governing themselves than any smaller class or body of men.

—Columbus, Ohio,
February 21, 1912

We, here in America, hold in our hands the hope of the world, the fate of the coming years; and shame and disgrace will be ours if in our eyes the light of high resolve is dimmed, if we trail in the dust the golden hopes of men.

—New York City, March 20, 1912

We stand against all tyranny, by the few or by the many.

Ibid.

Americans learn only from catastrophes and not from experience.

—An Autobiography, 1913

ART

After exploring an international exhibition of modern art, which included Marcel Duchamp's Nude Descending a Staircase:
There is in my bathroom a really good Navajo rug which, on any proper interpretation of the Cubist theory, is a far more satisfactory and decorative picture.

—The Outlook, March 29, 1913

The lunatic fringe was fully in evidence, especially in the rooms devoted to the Cubists and the Futurists, or Near-Impressionists.
Ibid.

The Cubists are entitled to the serious attention of all who find enjoyment in the puzzle-pictures of the Sunday newspapers.
Ibid.

There are thousands of people who will pay small sums to look at [P. T. Barnum's] faked mermaid, and now and then one of this kind with enough money will buy a Cubist picture, or a picture of a misshapen nude woman, repellent from every standpoint.
Ibid.

ASSASSINATION

Excepting in a crowd I do not think a bodyguard is the least use. Of course there is always the chance that a desperate man willing to give his own life may attack anyone under circumstances which will render him ... helpless. But if there is any chance to break even with a would-be assassin I think the man himself, if alert and resolute, has a better opportunity to defend himself than any bodyguard would have to defend him.

—Letter to ex-Rough Rider
William H. H. Llewellyn,
the White House,
October 19, 1901

No man will ever be restrained from becoming president by any fear as to his personal safety.

—First annual message to
Congress, December 3, 1901

BIG BUSINESS

We demand that big business give the people a square deal; in return we must insist that when anyone engaged in big business honestly endeavors to do right he shall himself be given a square deal.

—Letter to Sir Edward Gray,
November 15, 1913

BOATING

I cannot help thinking that the people with motor boats miss a great deal. If they would only keep to rowboats or canoes, and use oar or paddle … they would get infinitely more benefit than by having their work done for them by gasoline.

—*An Autobiography*, 1913

BOOKS

I hardly know whether to call it a bad book or not.

—Comment on Leo Tolstoy's
Anna Karenina, in a letter to sister
Corinne from Dickinson, Dakota
Territory, 1884

Tolstoi is a great writer. Do you notice how he never comments on the actions of his personages? He relates what they thought or did without any remark whatever as to whether it was good or bad, as Thucydides wrote history—a fact which tends to give his work an unmoral rather than an immoral tone.

Ibid.

BOOKS
[continued]

No man ever really learned from books how to manage a governmental system.… If he has never done anything but study books he will not be a statesman at all.

—*Atlantic Monthly*, August 1890

Normally I only care for a novel if the ending is good. I quite agree with you that if the hero has to die he ought to die worthily and nobly, so that our sorrow at the tragedy shall be tempered with the joy and pride one always feels when a man does his duty well and bravely.

—Letter to son Kermit, on the subject of the Charles Dickens novel *Nicholas Nickleby*, November 19, 1905

There is quite enough sorrow and shame and suffering and baseness in real life, and there is no need for meeting it unnecessarily in fiction.

Ibid.

Many learned people seem to feel that the quality of readableness in a book is one which warrants suspicion. Indeed, not a few learned people seem to feel that the fact that a book is interesting is proof that it is shallow.

—*History as Literature*, 1913

Books are almost as individual as friends.

—An Autobiography, 1913

The statesman, and the publicist, and the reformer, and the agitator for new things, and the upholder of what is good in old things, all need more than anything else to know human nature, to know the needs of the human soul; and they will find this nature and these needs set forth nowhere else but in the great imaginative writers, whether of prose or of poetry.

Ibid.

I am old fashioned, or sentimental, or something about books! Whenever I read one I want, in the first place, to enjoy myself, and, in the next place, to feel that I am a little better and not a little worse for having read it.

—Quoted in *Power and Responsibility*,
William Henry Harbaugh, 1961

BOXING

A boxer since his days at Harvard, Roosevelt encouraged it in the training of members of the New York police department when he was commissioner and advocated it as part of the character-development program of the Young Men's Christian Association and in the training of men for the army and navy. He boxed for exercise while governor of New York, but he imposed restraints on prize fighting in an effort to wipe out corruption. He boxed for exercise in the White House until an injury to his left eye persuaded him to give it up, although he did take up jujitsu.

BOXING

[continued]

I regard boxing, whether professional or amateur, as a first-class sport, and I do not regard it as brutalizing. Of course matches can be conducted under conditions that make them brutalizing. But this is true of football games and of most other rough and vigorous sports.

—*An Autobiography*, 1913

Most certainly prize-fighting is not half as brutalizing or demoralizing as many forms of big business and of the legal work carried on in connection with big business.

Ibid.

I shall always maintain that boxing contests themselves make good, healthy sport. It is idle to compare them to bull-fighting; the torture and death of the wretched horses in bull-fighting is enough of itself to blast the sport, no matter how great the skill and prowess shown by the bullfighters. Any sport in which the death and torture of animals is made to furnish pleasure to the spectators is debasing.

Ibid.

There should always be the opportunity provided in a glove fight or bare-fist fight to stop it when one competitor is hopelessly outclassed or too badly hammered.

Ibid.

The men who take part in these fights are hard as nails, and it is not worth while to feel sentimental about their receiving punishment which as a matter of fact they do not mind. Of course the men who look on ought to be able to stand up with the gloves, or without them, themselves; I have scant use for the type of sportsmanship which consists merely in looking on at the feats of someone else.

Ibid.

BULLYING

Bullies do not make brave men; and boys and men of foul life cannot become good citizens, good Americans, until they change; and even after the change, scars will be left on their souls.

—"The American Boy,"
St. Nicholas magazine, May 1900

A healthy-minded boy should feel hearty contempt for the coward and even more hearty indignation for the boy who bullies girls or small boys, or tortures animals.

Ibid.

Every good boy should have it in him to thrash the objectional boy as the need arises.

Ibid.

BULLYING
[continued]

I abhor injustice and bullying by the strong at the expense of the weak.

—An Autobiography, 1913

CHARACTER

It is always better to be an original than an imitation.

—Forum, April 1894

Bodily vigor is good, and vigor of intellect is even better, but far above is character.

—"Character and Success,"
The Outlook, March 31, 1900

In the great battle of life, no brilliancy of intellect, no perfection of bodily development, will count when weighed in the balance against that assemblage of virtues, active and passive, of moral qualities which we group together under the name of character.

Ibid.

It is character that counts in a nation as in a man.

—Galena, Illinois, April 27, 1900

There are good men and bad men of all nationalities, creeds and colors; and if this world of ours is ever to become what we hope some day it may become, it must be by the general recognition that the man's heart and soul, the man's worth and actions, determine his standing.

—Letter, Oyster Bay, New York,
September 1, 1903

Let the watchwords of all our people be the old familiar watchwords of honesty, decency, fair-dealing, and common-sense.

—New York State Fair, Syracuse,
September 7, 1903

A man may neglect his political duties because he is lazy, too selfish, too short-sighted, or too timid; but whatever the reason may be it is certainly an unworthy reason, and it shows either a weakness or worse than a weakness in the man's character.

—Address to Harvard Union,
Harvard University,
Cambridge, Massachusetts,
February 23, 1907

Character is far more important than intellect in making a man a good citizen or successful at his calling—meaning by character not only such qualities as honesty and truthfulness, but courage, perseverance and self-reliance.

—*North American Review*,
August 1890

CHARACTER
[continued]

If a man does not have an ideal and try to live up to it, then he becomes a mean, base and sordid creature, no matter how successful.

> —Letter to his son Kermit, quoted in
> *Theodore Roosevelt*,
> Joseph Bucklin Bishop, 1915

Unless a man is master of his soul, all other kinds of mastery amount to little.

> —*Ladies' Home Journal*, January 1917

CHILDREN

In a Christmastime 1898 talk to school children in Oyster Bay, New York, TR offered this advice on how to get along in life:

Don't let anyone impose on you. Don't be quarrelsome, but stand up for your rights. If you've got to fight, fight and fight hard and well. To my mind, a coward is the only thing meaner than a liar.

There are two things that I want you to make up your minds to: first, that you are going to have a good time as long as you live—I have no use for the sour-faced man—and next, that you are going to do something worth while, that you are going to work hard and do the things you set out to do.

Ibid.

Example is the most potent of all things.

—Speech to Holy Name Society,
Oyster Bay, New York,
August 16, 1903

It is no use to preach to [children] if you do not act decently yourself.

Ibid.

The father, the elder brothers, the friends can do much toward seeing that boys as they become men become clean and honorable men.

Ibid.

What we have a right to expect of the American boy is that he shall turn out to be a good American man.

—"The American Boy,"
St. Nicholas magazine, May 1900

He must not be a coward or a weakling, a bully, a shirk, or a prig. He must work hard and play hard. He must be clean-minded and clean-lived, and able to hold his own under all circumstances and against all comers.

Ibid.

CHILDREN
[continued]

Children are better than books.

—*An Autobiography*, 1913

For unflagging interest and enjoyment, a household of children, if things go reasonably well, certainly makes all other forms of success and achievement lose their importance by comparison.

Ibid.

The country is the place for children, and if not in the country, a city small enough so that one can get into the country.

Ibid.

I never keep boys waiting. It's a hard trial for a boy to wait.

—Quoted in *Theodore Roosevelt, a Life*, Nathan Miller, 1992

The one thing I want to leave my children is an honorable name.

—Quoted in *Power and Responsibility*, William Henry Harbaugh, 1961

CITIZENSHIP

It ought to be axiomatic in this country that every man must devote a reasonable share of his time to doing his duty in the political life of the community.

—*Forum*, July 1894

The average citizen must devote a great deal of thought and time to the affairs of the State, and he must devote that thought and that time steadily and intelligently.

—Boston, August 25, 1902

The first requisite of a good citizen in this Republic of ours is that he shall be able and willing to pull his weight.

—New York City,
November 11, 1902

The good citizen is the man who, whatever his wealth or his poverty, strives manfully to do his duty to himself, to his family, to his neighbor, to the state; who is incapable of the baseness which manifests itself either in arrogance or envy, but who while demanding justice for himself is no less scrupulous to offer justice to others.

—New York State Fair, Syracuse,
September 7, 1903

COMMON SENSE

There is … one quality which perhaps, strictly speaking, is as much intellectual as moral, but which is too often wholly lacking in men of high intellectual ability, and without which real character cannot exist—namely, the fundamental gift of commonsense.

—*The Outlook*, November 8, 1913

COMPROMISE

No student of American history needs to be reminded that the Constitution itself is a bundle of compromises.

—*Atlantic Monthly*, August 1894

Now and then one can stand uncompromisingly for a naked principle and force people up to it. This is always the attractive course; but in certain great crises it may be the wrong course.

Ibid.

A compromise which results in a half-step toward evil is all wrong.

Ibid.

COMPROMISE
[continued]

Self-governing free men must have the power to accept
necessary compromises, to make necessary concessions, each
sacrificing somewhat of prejudice, even of principle, and every
group must show the necessary subordination of its particular
interests of the community as a whole.

—*Oliver Cromwell*, 1900

Public men have great temptations. They are always
obliged to compromise in order to do anything at all.

—Quoted in *The Republican Roosevelt*,
John Morton Blum, 1954

CONGRESS

The history of free government is in large part the history
of those representative bodies in which, from the earliest
times, free government has found its loftiest expression.… A
leading part therein must be taken by this august and powerful
legislative body over which I have been called upon to preside.

—Inaugural address as vice president,
and thereby president of the U.S.
Senate, the Capitol,
Washington, D.C., March 4, 1901

I took the [Panama] canal zone and let Congress debate, and while the debate goes on the canal does also.

—Berkeley, California,
March 23, 1911

In domestic politics Congress in the long run is apt to do what is right. It is in foreign politics, and in preparing the army and navy that we are apt to have most difficulty, because these are just the subjects as to which the average American citizen does not take the trouble to think carefully or deeply.

—Quoted in *The Republican Roosevelt*,
John Morton Blum, 1954

CONSERVATION

It is not what we have that will make us a great nation; it is the way in which we use it.

—Dickinson, Dakota Territory,
July 4, 1886

More and more, as it becomes necessary to preserve the game, let us hope that the camera will largely supplant the rifle.

—Oyster Bay, New York,
May 31, 1901

CONSERVATION
[continued]

We of the older generation can get along with what we have, though with growing hardship, but in your full manhood and womanhood you will want what nature once so beautifully supplied and man so thoughtlessly destroyed; and because of that want you will reproach us, not for what we have used, but for what we have wasted.... So any nation which in its youth lives only for the day, reaps without sowing, and consumes without husbanding, must expect the penalty of the prodigal whose labor could with difficulty find him the bare means of life.

—Arbor Day, April 15, 1907

To waste, to destroy, our natural resources, to skin and exhaust the land instead of using it so as to increase its usefulness, will result in undermining in the days of our children the very prosperity which we ought by right to hand down to them amplified and developed.

—Message to Congress,
December 3, 1907

The conservation of our natural resources and their proper use constitute the fundamental problem which underlies almost every other problem of our national life.

—Jamestown, Virginia, June 10, 1907

CONSERVATION
[continued]

It is time for us now as a nation to exercise the same reasonable foresight in dealing with our great national resources that would be shown by any prudent man in conserving and wisely using the property which contains the assurance of well-being for himself and his children.

> —Conference on the Conservation of
> Natural Resources,
> the White House, May 13, 1908

Conservation means development as much as it does protection. I recognize the right and duty of this generation to develop and use the natural resources of our land; but I do not recognize the right to waste them, or to rob, by wasteful use, the generations that come after us.

> —Osawatomie, Kansas,
> August 31, 1910

There can be nothing in the world more beautiful than the Yosemite, the groves of the giant sequoias and redwoods, the Canyon of the Colorado, the Canyon of the Yellowstone, the Three Tetons; and our people should see to it that they are preserved for their children and their children's children forever, with their majestic beauty all unmarred.

> —*Outdoor Pastimes of an American*
> *Hunter*, 1905

CONSERVATIVES

The only true conservative is the man who resolutely sets his face toward the future.

—Quoted in *The Republican Roosevelt*,
John Morton Blum, 1954

COOPERATION

All for each, and each for all, is a good motto, but only on condition that each works with might and main to so maintain himself as not to be a burden to others.

—*An Autobiography*, 1913

CORRUPTION

There is no greater duty than to war on the corrupt and unprincipled [political] boss, and on the corrupt and unprincipled business man; and for that matter, the corrupt and unprincipled labor leader also, and on the corrupt and unprincipled editor, and on any one else who is corrupt and unprincipled.

—*An Autobiography*, 1913

COURAGE

The man who, in the long run, will count for most in bettering municipal life is the man who actually steps down into the hurly-burly, who is not frightened by the sweat and the blood, and the blows of friends and foes; who haunts not the fringy edges of the fight, but the pell-mell of men.

—*The Outlook*, December 21, 1895

Good weapons are necessary, but if you put the best weapon that can be invented into the hands of a coward, he will be beaten by a brave man with a club.

—Kansas City, Missouri, May 1, 1903

Courtesy is as much a mark of a gentleman as courage.

—*The Outlook*, April 1, 1911

Three-o'clock-in-the-morning courage is the most desirable kind.

—*An Autobiography*, 1913

CRIMINALITY

In criminality comes the life of mere vapid ease, the ignoble life of a man who desires nothing from his years but that they shall be led with the least effort, the least trouble, the greatest amount of physical enjoyment—or intellectual enjoyment of a mere dilettante type.

—Groton, Massachusetts,
May 24, 1904

CRISES

At times a great crisis comes in which a great people, perchance led by a great man, can … make a long stride in advance along the path of justice and orderly liberty.

—Providence, Rhode Island,
August 23, 1902

There is a certain tendency among excellent people to believe that everything can be accomplished by law; that when there is any wrong, it is due to what they call the state of society, and that there is immediate need for radical and sweeping changes in the social system.

—Kansas City, Missouri, May 1, 1903

CRISES

[continued]

There is little use for the being whose tepid soul knows nothing of the great and generous emotion, of the high pride, the stern belief, the lofty enthusiasm, of the men who quell the storm and ride the thunder.

—Sorbonne, Paris, France,
April 23, 1910

The men who have made our national greatness are those who faced danger and overcame it, who met difficulties and surmounted them, not those whose lines were cast in such pleasant places that toil and dread were ever far from them.

—Galena, Illinois, June 17, 1912

DARING

Far better it is to dare mighty things, to win glorious triumphs, even though checkered by failure, than to take rank with those poor spirits who neither enjoy much nor suffer much, because they live in the gray twilight that knows not victory nor defeat.

—Hamilton Club, Chicago, Illinois,
April 10, 1899

DEATH

Death is always and under all circumstances a tragedy, for if it is not, then it means that life itself has become one.

> —Letter to Cecil Spring-Rice,
> March 12, 1900

No brave and good man can properly shirk death; and no criminal who has earned death should be allowed to shirk it.

> —*An Autobiography*, 1913

DEBATING

I have not the slightest sympathy with debating contests in which each side is arbitrarily assigned a given proposition and told to maintain it without the least reference to whether they believe in it or not. What we need is to turn out of our colleges young men with ardent convictions on the side of the right; not young men who can make good arguments for either right or wrong, as their interest bids them.

> —Quoted in *Theodore Roosevelt,*
> *Strenuous American,*
> Alvin F. Harlow, 1943

DEMAGOGUES

To play the demagogue for purposes of self-interest is a cardinal sin against the people in a democracy.

—*An Autobiography*, 1913

DEMOCRACY

Our country offers the most wonderful example of democratic government on a giant scale that the world has ever seen; and the peoples of the world are watching to see whether we succeed or fail.

—Saratoga, New York,
September 27, 1910

We believe in all our hearts in democracy; in the capacity of the people to govern themselves; and we are bound to succeed, for our success means not only our own triumph, but the triumph of the cause of the rights of the people throughout the world, and the uplifting of the banner of hope for all the nations of mankind.

Ibid.

DEMOCRACY
[continued]

A great democracy must be progressive or it will soon cease to be a great democracy.

> —Quoted by President Franklin D. Roosevelt, TR's cousin, at the dedication of the Theodore Roosevelt Memorial, New York City, January 20, 1936

DESTINY

We are face to face with our destiny and we must meet it with a high and resolute courage.

> —Quoted in book jacket note, *Ambulance No. 10—Personal Letters from the Front*, Leslie Buswell, 1918

DETECTIVES

There are certain kinds of crime which can be reached only by the use of detective methods—gamblers, keepers of disorderly houses and law-breaking liquor dealers can hardly ever be touched otherwise. It would be almost useless to try to enforce the law against any of them if we continued to employ [only] uniformed people.

—*Atlantic Monthly*, August 1897

The man with the nightstick, the man in the blue coat with the helmet, can keep order and repress open violence on the streets; but most kinds of crime are ordinarily carried on furtively and stealthily—perhaps at night, perhaps behind closed doors. It is possible to reach them only by the employment of the man in plain clothes, the detective.

Ibid.

DIPLOMACY

Diplomacy is utterly useless where there is no force behind it; the diplomat is the servant, not the master, of the soldier.

—Newport, Rhode Island,
June 2, 1897

DISCIPLINE

We need discipline for our boys. We need discipline for our men. We need discipline in our own individual characters. We need it if we are going to be any use to ourselves; and we need it unless we expect to be quite intolerable to others.

—*Ladies' Home Journal*, January 1917

DUTY

I honor beyond measure those who do their full duty ... and all the more because the doing of duty generally means pain, hardship, self-mastery, self-denial, endurance of risk, of labor, of irksome monotony, wearing effort, steady perseverance under difficulty and discouragement.

—Letter, Oyster Bay, New York,
July 19, 1903

If only we can make the man or the woman who, in the home or out of the home, does well his or her hard duty, feel that at least there is a recognition of respect because of that duty being well performed, we shall be by just so much ahead as a nation.

—Letter to John Hay, August 9, 1903

In the long fight for righteousness the watchword for all of us is spend and be spent. It is little matter whether any one man fails or succeeds; but the cause shall not fail, for it is the cause of mankind.

—New York City, March 20, 1912

The performance of duty, and not an indulgence in vapid ease and vapid pleasure, is all that makes life worth while.

—*An Autobiography*, 1913

EDUCATION

The man with the university education is in honor bound to take an active part in our political life, and to do his full duty as a citizen by helping his fellow citizens to the extent of his power in the exercise of the rights of self-government.

—*Atlantic Monthly*, August 1890

There is superstition in science quite as much as there is superstition in theology, and it is all the more dangerous because those suffering from it are profoundly convinced that they are freeing themselves from all superstition.

—*The Outlook*, December 12, 1911

EDUCATION
[continued]

From the standpoint of the nation, and from the broader standpoint of mankind, scholarship is of worth chiefly when it is productive, when the scholar not merely receives or acquires, but gives.

—*The Outlook*, January 13, 1912

EFFICIENCY

If a man's efficiency is not guided and regulated by a moral sense, then the more efficient he is ... the more dangerous to the body politic.

—Sorbonne, Paris, France,
April 23, 1910

National efficiency ... is a necessary result of the principle of conservation widely applied. In the end it will determine our failure or success as a nation. National efficiency has to do not only with natural resources and with men but it is equally concerned with institutions. The state must be made efficient for the work which concerns only the people of the state; and the nation for that which concerns all the people.

—Speech, "The New Nationalism,"
Osawatomie, Kansas,
August 31, 1910, and published in
The New Nationalism, 1910

ENVY

Envy is as evil a thing as arrogance.

—Letter, Oyster Bay, New York,
September 1, 1903

EQUAL OPPORTUNITY

All that the law can do is to shape things that no injustice shall be done by one to the other, and that each man shall be given the first chance to show the stuff there is in him.

—Kansas City, Missouri, May 1, 1903

In every wise struggle for human betterment one of the main objects, and often the only object, has been to achieve in large measure equality of opportunity.

—Osawatomie, Kansas,
August 31, 1910

The humblest among us, no matter what his creed, his birthplace, or the color of his skin, so long as he behaves in a straight and decent fashion, must have guaranteed to him under the law his right to life and liberty, to protection from injustice, to the enjoyment of the fruits of his own labor, and

EFFICIENCY
[continued]

to do his share in the work of self-government on the same terms with others of like fitness.

—*The Outlook*, August 24, 1912

It is in my mind equally an outrage ... to appoint an improper man to a position because he is a Negro, or with a view of affecting the Negro vote, or on the other hand, to exclude a proper man from an office ... because he is a Negro. I shall never knowingly consent to either doctrine.

—Quoted in *The Republican Roosevelt*, John Morton Blum, 1954

EVIL

War with evil; but show no spirit of malignity toward the man who may be responsible for the evil. Put it out of his power to do wrong.

—Oyster Bay, New York, July 4, 1906

Measure iniquity by the heart, whether a man's purse be full or empty, partly full or partly empty. If the man is a decent man, whether well off or not well off, stand by him; if he is not a decent man stand against him, whether he be rich or poor.

Ibid.

EVIL

[continued]

The worst of all lives is the vicious life; the life of a man who becomes a positive addition to the forces of evil in a community.

—Chicago, Illinois, June 17, 1912

EXERCISE

I wish to preach, not the doctrine of ignoble ease, but the doctrine of the strenuous life.

—Hamilton Club, Chicago, Illinois,
April 10, 1899

There is a danger that the mere office man ... who does not take part in rough game and rough play outside ... will become a wretched routine creature, adept only in the pedantry of his profession and apt to come to an unexpected disaster.

—Letter, Oyster Bay, New York,
July 19, 1902

Personally I have always felt that I might serve as an object lesson as to the benefit of good hard bodily exercise to the ordinary man. I never was a champion at anything. I have never fenced.... I was fond of boxing and fairly good at it. I was a fair rider, a fair rifle shot, and possessing the ordinary hardihood and endurance of the out-of-door man I have done a good deal of work in the wilderness after big game. Of late years, since I have been Governor of New York and afterwards President, my life has necessarily been very sedentary; but I have certain playmates among my friends here in Washington and with those I take occasional long walks, or rather scrambles, through the woods and over the rocks.

—Letter, June 15, 1903

We're not building anything this afternoon. Something is coming down. It's bully exercise.

—Sagamore Hill, Oyster Bay,
New York, summer 1904,
inviting a friend to join him in
cutting down some brush and trees.

Editor's Note: Not until the presidency of Ronald Reagan in the 1980s would Americans see so many photographs of a president wielding an ax.

A man whose business is sedentary should get some kind of exercise if he wishes to keep himself in as good physical trim as his brethren who do manual labor.

—*An Autobiography*, 1913

EXERCISE
[continued]

I rarely took exercise merely as exercise. Primarily I took it because I liked it.

Ibid.

The dweller in cities has less chance than the dweller in the country to keep his body sound and vigorous. But he can do so, if only he will take the trouble.

Ibid.

EXTREMISM

Quack remedies of the universal cure-all type are generally as noxious to the body politic as to the body corporal.

—*Review of Reviews*, January 1897

While extremists are sometimes men who are in advance of their age, more often they are men who are not in advance at all, but simply to one side or the other of a great movement, or even lagging behind it, or trying to pilot it in the wrong direction.

—*Oliver Cromwell*, 1900

EYES ON THE STARS

Be practical as well as generous in your ideals. Keep your eyes on the stars, but remember to keep your feet on the ground.

—The Groton School, Groton,
Massachusetts, May 24, 1904

It is true of the Nation, as of the individual, that the greatest doer must also be a great dreamer.

—Berkeley, California, 1911

FAILURE

It is hard to fail, but it is worse never to have tried to succeed.

—Chicago, Illinois, April 10, 1899

FAMILY

A man must be a good husband, and father, a woman, a good daughter, wife and mother, first and foremost.

—New York City, December 30, 1900

FAMILY

[continued]

In a family, the father and mother who fail to rear their sons and daughters to recognize and perform their duties neither receive nor deserve the loyal devotion felt for the heads of the household where the whole household is trained to put duty ahead of pleasure.

—*The New York Times*,
September 10, 1917

FEAR

There were all kinds of things I was afraid of at first, ranging from grizzly bears to "mean" horses and gun-fighters; but by acting as if I was not afraid I gradually ceased to be afraid.

—*An Autobiography*, 1913

The worst of all fears is the fear of living.

Ibid.

FIGHTING

Don't hit at all if you can help it; don't hit a man if you can possibly avoid it; but if you do hit him, put him to sleep.

—New York City, February 17, 1899

One learns fast in a fight.

—*An Autobiography*, 1913

The loose tongue and the unready hand make a poor combination.

—Oyster Bay, New York, July 7, 1915

The only proper rule is never fight at all if you can honorably avoid it, but never under any circumstances to fight in a half-hearted way.

—*Foes of Our Own Household*, 1917

FOOTBALL

To borrow a simile from the football field, we believe that men must play fair, but that there must be no shirking, and that the success can only come to the player who "hits the line hard."

—Sagamore Hill, Oyster Bay, New York, October 1897

FOOTBALL
[continued]

I do not in the least object to your getting smashed if it is for an object that is worth while, such as playing on the Groton [football] team or playing on your class team when you get to Harvard. But I think it is a little silly to run any imminent risk of a serious smash simply to play on the second squad instead of the third.

—Letter to son Ted,
October 11, 1903

I am delighted to have you play football. I believe in rough, manly sports. But I do not believe in them if they degenerate into the sole end of any one's existence. I do not want you to sacrifice standing well in your studies to any over-athleticism; and I need not tell you that character counts for a great deal more than either intellect or body in winning success in life.

—Letter to son Ted, quoted in
Theodore Roosevelt, Strenuous American, Alvin F. Harlow, 1943

If an individual starts to play football, and expects not to get bumped, he will be sadly disappointed.

—Address at Occidental College,
Los Angeles, California,
March 22, 1911

FOREIGN RELATIONS

More and more the increasing interdependence and complexity of international political and economic relations render it incumbent on all civilized and orderly powers to insist on the proper policing of the world.

—Address to Congress, 1902

Let us speak courteously, deal fairly, and keep ourselves armed and ready.

—San Francisco, California,
May 13, 1903

Much has been given us, and much will rightfully be expected from us. We have duties to others and duties to ourselves; and we can shirk neither. We have become a great nation, forced by the fact of its greatness into relations with the other nations of the earth, and we must behave as beseems a people with such responsibilities.

—Presidential inaugural address,
the Capitol, Washington, D.C.,
March 4, 1905

FOREIGN RELATIONS
[continued]

It is essential that we should have it clearly understood, by our own people especially, but also by other peoples, that the Pacific was as much our home waters as the Atlantic.

> —*An Autobiography*, 1913, on sending
> "the White Fleet" of the U.S. Navy
> on an around-the-world cruise

The most important service I rendered to peace was the voyage of the battle fleet round the world.

> Ibid.

Each nation must keep well prepared to defend itself until the establishment of some form of international police power, competent and willing to prevent violence as between nations.

> —Christiania, Norway, May 5, 1910

The United States of America has not the option as to whether it will or will not play a great part in the world. It *must* play a great part.

> —*The Outlook*, April 1, 1911

We must so conduct ourselves that every big nation and every little nation that behaves itself shall never have to think of us with fear, and shall have confidence not only in our justice but in our courtesy.

—*The Outlook*, September 23, 1914

In 1914, while advocating strengthening of national defenses in the face of the war in Europe, the former president of the United States appeared to be looking beyond the current crisis and predicting not only the second world war, but also the Cold War with the Soviet Union, the organization of a western alliance in the form of the North Atlantic Treaty Organization (NATO), and a rebuilding of Germany as a bulwark against communist expansion:

I see no reason for believing that Russia is more advanced than Germany as regards international ethics, and Japan, with all her politeness and her veneer of western civilization, is at heart delighted to attack any and every western nation whenever the chances come and there is an opportunity for Japan to gain what she desires with reasonable safety. If Germany is smashed, it is perfectly possible that later she will have to be supported as a bulwark against [Russia] by the nations of Western Europe.

Ibid.

It is by no means necessary that a great nation should always stand at the heroic level. But no nation has the root of greatness in it unless in time of need it can rise to the heroic mood.

—*Fear God and Take Your Own Part*, 1916

FRIENDSHIP

If a man has a very decided character, has a strongly accentuated career, it is normally the case ... that he makes ardent friends and bitter enemies.

—Quoted in *Power and Responsibility*,
William Henry Harbaugh, 1961

GOVERNMENT

Honesty and common sense are the two prime requisites for a legislator.

—Albany, New York, 1883

The bulk of government is not legislation but administration.

—Quoted in *The Republican Roosevelt*,
John Morton Blum, 1954

Abundant revenues and a large surplus always invite extravagance, and constant care should be taken to guard against unnecessary increase of the ordinary expenses of government.

—Fourth annual message to
Congress, December 6, 1904

Men can never escape being governed. Either they must govern themselves or they must submit to being governed by others.

—Jamestown, Virginia, April 26, 1907

The object of government is the welfare of the people.

—*The New Nationalism*, 1910

Unless this is in very truth a government of, by, and for the people, then both historically and in world interest our national existence loses most of its point.

—*The Outlook*, Jan. 21, 1911

You cannot give self-government to anybody.

—Madison, Wisconsin, April 15, 1911

All of us, you and I, all of us together, want to rule ourselves, and we don't wish to have any body of outsiders rule us. That is what free government means.

—St. Louis, Missouri,
March 28, 1912

We, the people, rule ourselves, and what we really want from our representatives is that they shall manage the government for us along the lines we lay down, and shall do this with efficiency and good faith.

Ibid.

GREATNESS

We cannot do great deeds unless we are willing to do the small things that make up the sum of greatness.

—New York, New York,
May 30, 1899

GUNBOAT DIPLOMACY

On December 16, 1907, sixteen battleships known as the Great White Fleet set sail from Hampton Roads, Virginia, for a round-the-world cruise to show the flag and demonstrate that the United States was a world naval power:

Did you ever see such a fleet and such a day? By George, isn't it magnificent?

—Aboard the presidential yacht
Mayflower, December 16, 1907

No foreign country expected that we could send that battle fleet around the world in the shape in which we sent it, because none of the foreign countries of the greatest naval power believed that they themselves could do it; and they were proportionally impressed not only by the fact that we did it but by the way in which it was done—by the fact that the fleet, after being away for a year and a quarter, and circumnavigating the globe, came back, having kept to the minute every

GUNBOAT DIPLOMACY
[continued]

appointment on its schedule, and reached home in far better fighting trim as regards both men and ships than when it sailed. That impressed all responsible statesmen abroad much more keenly even than it impressed our own people.

—Harvard University, Cambridge,
Massachusetts, December 14, 1910

HAPPINESS

Happiness cannot come to any man capable of enjoying true happiness unless it comes as the sequel to duty well and honestly done.

—The Groton School, Groton,
Massachusetts, May 24, 1904

If you have small, shallow souls, shallow souls and shallow hearts, I will not say you will be unhappy; you can obtain the bridge-club standards of happiness; and you can go through life without cares and without sorrows, and without conscious effort, in so far as your brains will enable you to do so; but you have richly deserved the contempt of everybody whose respect is worth having.

—Address at Occidental College,
Los Angeles, California,
March 22, 1911

HELPING HAND

There is not a man of us ... who does not at times need a helping hand to be stretched out to him, and then shame upon him who will not stretch out the helping hand to his brother.

—Pasadena, California, May 8, 1903

The welfare of each of us is dependent fundamentally upon the welfare of all of us.

—New York State Fair, Syracuse,
September 7, 1903

None of us can really prosper permanently if masses of our fellows are debased and degraded, if they are ground down and forced to live starved and sordid lives, so that their souls are crippled like their bodies and the fine edge of their feeling blunted.

—Chicago, Illinois, June 17, 1912

This country will not be a permanently good place for any of us to live in unless we make it a reasonably good place for all of us to live in.

Ibid.

HEROISM

Every feat of heroism makes us forever indebted to the man who performed it.

—Newport, Rhode Island,
June 2, 1897

All daring and courage, all iron endurance of misfortune, all devotion to the ideal of honor and of the glory of the flag, make for a finer and nobler type of manhood.

Ibid.

In July 1918, when the youngest Roosevelt son, Quentin, an aviator in France, was reported to have been shot down and un-accounted for, TR inserted the following remarks into an address to the Republican State Convention in Saratoga, New York:
The finest, the bravest, the best of our young men have sprung eagerly forward to face death for the sake of a high ideal, and thereby they have brought home to us the great truth that life consists of more than easygoing pleasure, and more than hard, conscienceless, brutal striving after purely material success; that while we must rightly care for the body and the things of the body, yet that such care leads nowhere unless we also have thought that for our own souls and for the souls of our brothers. When these gallant boys, on the golden crest of life, gladly face death for the sake of an ideal, shall not

we, who stay behind, who have not been found worthy of the great adventure, shall we not in turn try to shape our lives, so as to make in this country a better place to live in for these men, and for the woman who sent these men to battle and for the children who are to come after them?

After Quentin was found dead and was buried where his plane had gone down, TR wrote to son Archie:

Well, it is very dreadful, but, after all, he died as the heroes of old died; as brave and fearless men must die when a great cause calls. If our country did not contain such men it would not be our country.

—Quoted in *The Roosevelt Family of Sagamore Hill*, Hermann Hagedorn, 1954

HIMSELF

I fight when I am attacked.

—New York City Hall, May 5, 1896

I am as strong as a bull moose and you can use me to the limit.

—Letter to Republican leader Mark Hanna in answer to the question of whether TR was available to run for vice president of the United States, June 17, 1900

HIMSELF
[continued]

In October 1901 when TR invited Booker T. Washington to a
dinner (the first black man to dine at the White House) TR was sur-
prised and shocked by the outraged reaction to the invitation:

It never entered my head that any human being would so
much as comment upon it; for it seemed entirely obvious and
natural to show Booker Washington a little ordinary courtesy,
as I was consulting and advising with him on public policies of
real importance.

—Letter, October 25, 1901

When I asked Booker T. Washington to dinner I did not
devote very much thought to the matter one way or the other,
I respect him greatly and believe in the work he has done. I
have consulted so much with him it seemed to me that it was
natural to ask him to dinner to talk over his work, and the very
fact that I felt a moment's qualm on inviting him because of
his color made me ashamed of myself and made me hasten to
send the invitation. I did not think of its bearing one way or
the other either on my own future or in anything else. As
things have turned out, I am very glad that I asked him, for the
clamor aroused by the act makes me feel as if the act was
necessary.

—Letter, November 8, 1901

I preach the gospel of hope.

—Detroit, Michigan,
September 22, 1902

When I was young and rode across country I was light and tough, and if I did, as actually happened, break an arm or a rib no damage ensued and no scandal was caused. Now I am stiff and heavy, and any accident to me would cause immense talk, and I do not take the chance; simply because it is not worth while.

—Letter to son Ted,
October 11, 1903

My hat's in the ring. The fight is on and I'm stripped to the buff.

—Press conference, 1912

When Owen Wister, during a visit to TR at the White House, chided TR for not maintaining more control over TR's rambunctious teenage daughter Alice, TR answered:

I can do one of two things. I can be President of the United States, or I can control Alice. I cannot possibly do both.

—*Roosevelt, the Story of a Friendship*,
Owen Wister, 1930

The great bulk of my wealthy and educated friends regard me as a dangerous crank.

—Summer 1912, quoted in *The Roosevelt Family of Sagamore Hill*,
Hermann Hagedorn, 1954

HIMSELF
[continued]

While TR was running as an independent candidate for president of the United States on the Bullmoose Party ticket in 1912, a half-crazed fanatic shot him in the chest as he was leaving his hotel in Milwaukee, Wisconsin, to make a speech. Although seriously wounded and with the bullet still in him, TR refused to be taken to a hospital. He demanded, "You get me to that speech. It may be the last I shall deliver, but I am going to deliver it." He spoke for an hour and a half. During the speech, as an effort was made to persuade him to stop and go to the hospital, he told the audience:

Don't you waste any sympathy on me. I have had an A-1 time in life and I am having it now.

When he finished the speech he rejected being put on a waiting stretcher, declaring:

I'll not go to the hospital lying on that thing. I'll walk to the ambulance, and I'll walk from it to the hospital. I'm no weakling to be crippled by a flesh wound.

I did not care a rap for being shot. It is a trade risk, which every prominent public man ought to accept as a matter of course. For eleven years I have been prepared any day to be shot.

—Letter to Cecil Spring-Rice, 1912, quoted in *The Roosevelt Family of Sagamore Hill*, Hermann Hagedorn, 1954

Whenever there is tyranny by the majority I shall certainly fight it.

—St. Louis, Missouri,
March 28, 1912

I am not trying to be subtle or original. I am trying to make the plain everyday citizen here in America stand for the things which I regard as essential to good government.

—*Ladies' Home Journal*, October 1916

I have only a second rate brain, but I think I have a capacity for action.

—Quoted in *Roosevelt, the Story of a Friendship*, Owen Wister, 1930

I keep my good health by having a very bad temper, kept under good control.

—Remark to friends, 1917, quoted in *The Roosevelt Family of Sagamore Hill*, Hermann Hagedorn, 1954

I had just one more chance to be a boy, and I took it!

—Reply to a friend who asked TR why he had risked his life (and nearly died) on an expedition into an unexplored river in Brazil

HISTORY

The true historian will bring the past before our eyes as if it were present. He will make us see as living men the hard-faced archers of Agincourt, and the war-worn spearmen who followed Alexander down beyond the rim of the known world.…We shall also see the supreme righteousness of the wars for freedom and justice, and know that the men who fell in those wars made all mankind their debtors.

—American Historical Association,
December 17, 1912

History, taught for a directly and immediately useful purpose to pupils and the teachers of pupils, is one of the necessary features of a sound education in democratic citizenship.

—*History as Literature and Other Essays*, 1913

The vision of the great historian must be both wide and lofty.

Ibid.

The great speeches of statesmen and the great writings of historians can live only if they possess the deathless quality that inheres in all great literature.

Ibid.

HOME

When home ties are loosened; when men and women cease to regard a worthy family life, with all its duties fully performed, and all its responsibilities lived up to, as the life best worth living; then evil days for the commonwealth are at hand.

—Sixth annual message to Congress,
December 3, 1906

It is impossible to win the great prizes of life without running risks, and the greatest of all prizes are those connected to the home.

—*An Autobiography*, 1913

HONESTY

We can as little afford to tolerate a dishonest man in the public service as a coward in the army.

—Washington, D.C.,
October 15, 1903

HONESTY

[continued]

Be truthful; a lie implies fear, vanity, or malevolence; be frank; furtiveness and insincerity are faults incompatible with true manliness. Be honest, and remember that honesty counts for nothing unless back of it lie courage and efficiency.

—The Groton School, Groton,
Massachusetts, May 24, 1904

This country has nothing to fear from the crooked man who fails. We put him in jail. It is the crooked man who succeeds who is a threat to this country.

—Memphis, Tennessee,
October 25, 1905

You cannot have honesty in public life unless the average citizen demands honesty in public life.

—Chicago, Illinois,
September 8, 1910

HONOR

The man who makes a promise which he does not intend to keep, and does not try to keep, should rightly be ajudged to have forfeited in some degree what should be every man's most precious possession—his honor.

—San Francisco, California,
May 14, 1903

HUMAN RIGHTS

Arrogance, suspicion, brutal envy of the well-to-do, brutal indifference toward those who are not well-to-do, the hard refusal to consider the rights of others, the foolish refusal to consider the limits of beneficent action, the base appeal to the spirit of selfish greed, whether it take the form of plunder of the fortunate or of oppression of the unfortunate—from these and from all kindred vices this Nation must be kept free if it is to remain in its present position in the forefront of the peoples of mankind.

—Speech to the Chamber of
Commerce, New York City,
November 11, 1902

The man who wrongfully holds that every human right is secondary to his profit must now give way to the advocate of human welfare, who rightly maintains that every man holds his property subject to the general right of the community to regulate its use to whatever degree the public welfare may require it.

—*The New Nationalism*, 1910

HUNTING

In after-years there shall come forever to [the hunter's] mind the memory of the endless prairies shimmering in the bright sun; of vast snow-clad wastes lying desolate under gray skies; of the melancholy marches, of the rush of mighty rivers; of the breath of the evergreen forest in summer; of the crooning of ice-armored pines at the touch of winter.

—*The Wilderness Hunter*, 1893

It is a good thing for a man to be forced to show self-reliance, resourcefulness in emergency, willingness to endure fatigue and hunger, and at need to face risk. Hunting is praiseworthy very much in proportion as it tends to develop these qualities.

—Preface to *The Master of the Game*, Edward, second duke of York. Dated, the White House, February 15, 1904

The free, self-reliant, adventurous life, with its rugged and stalwart democracy; the wild surroundings, the grand beauty of the scenery, the chance to study the ways and habits of the woodland creatures—all these unite to give to the career of the wilderness hunter its peculiar charm.

—Author's preface, *The Wilderness Hunter*, 1893

HUNTING
[continued]

Hardy outdoor sports, like hunting, are in themselves of no small value to the national character and should be encouraged in every way.

—An Autobiography

All kinds of other qualities, moral and physical, enter into being a good hunter, and especially a good hunter after dangerous game, just as all kinds of other qualities in addition to skill with the rifle enter into being a good soldier.

Ibid.

With dangerous game, after a fair degree of efficiency with the rifle has been attained, the prime requisites are cool judgment and that kind of nerve which consists in avoiding being rattled.

Ibid.

If the man has the right stuff in him, his will grows stronger and stronger with each exercise of it—and if he has not the right stuff in him he had better keep clear of dangerous game hunting, or indeed of any other form of sport or work in which there is bodily peril.

Ibid.

HYPHENATED AMERICANS

The one thing abhorrent to the powers above the earth and under them is the hyphenated American—the "German-American," the "Irish-American," or the "native American." Be Americans—pure and simple.

—Buffalo, New York,
September 10, 1895

There is no place for the hyphen in our citizenship.... We are a nation, not a hodge-podge of foreign nationalities. We are a people, and not a polyglot boarding house.

—"The Square Deal in
Americanism," 1918

Americanism means many things. It means equality of rights and, therefore, equality of duty and of obligation. It means service to a common country. It means loyalty to one flag, to our flag, the flag of all of us. It means that all of us guarantee the rights of each of us.... To divide along the lines of caste or creed is un-American.

— Washington, D.C., January 1917,
*Proceedings of the Congress of
Constructive Patriotism*

IDEALS

A man is worthless unless he has in him a lofty devotion to an ideal, and he is worthless also unless he strives to realize this ideal by practical methods.

—*The Outlook*, July 28, 1900

If you have an ideal only good while you sit at home, an ideal that nobody can live up to in outside life, examine it closely, and then cast it away.

—The Groton School, Groton,
Massachusetts, May 24, 1904

I have mighty little use for ethics that are applied with such inefficiency that no good results come.

—Harvard University, Cambridge,
Massachusetts, December 14, 1910

No nation ever amounted to anything if it did not have within its soul the power of fealty to a lofty ideal.

—Berkeley, California, 1913

JUJITSU

Wrestling is simply a sport with rules almost as conventional as those of tennis, while jujitsu is really meant for practice in killing or disabling your adversary.

—Letter to son Kermit,
February 24, 1905

JOURNALISM

Of all the forces that tend for evil in a great city like New York, probably none are so potent as the sensational papers. Until one had experienced them it is difficult to realize the reckless indifference to truth and decency displayed by papers such as the two that have the largest circulation in New York City [the *World* and the *Tribune*].

—*Atlantic Monthly*, August 1897

Expose crime and hunt down the criminal; but remember that, even in the case of crime, if it is attacked in sensational, lurid, and untruthful fashion, the attack may do more damage to the public mind than the crime itself.

—Washington, D.C., April 4, 1906

JOURNALISM
[continued]

Yellow journalism deifies the cult of the mendacious, the sensational, and the inane, and, throughout its wide but vapid field, does as much to vulgarize and degrade the popular taste, to weaken the popular character, and to dull the edge of the popular conscience, as any influence under which the country can suffer. These men sneer at the very idea of paying heed to the dictates of a sound morality; as one of their number has cynically put it, they are concerned merely with selling the public whatever the public will buy—a theory of conduct which would justify the existence of every keeper of an opium den, of every foul creature who ministers to the vices of mankind.

—Kansas City *Star*, 1912

JOY OF LIVING

With all my heart I believe in the joy of living; but those who achieve it do not seek it as an end in itself, but as a seized and prized incident of hard work well done and of risk and danger never wantonly courted, but never shirked when duty commands that they be faced.

—*The Great Adventure*, 1918

From the largest to the smallest, happiness and usefulness are largely found in the same souls, and the joy of life is won in its deepest and truest sense only by those who have not shirked life's burdens.

—Syracuse, New York,
September 7, 1903

At Sagamore Hill we love a great many things—birds and trees and books, and all things beautiful, and horses and rifles and children and hard work and the joy of life.

—*An Autobiography*, 1913

JUDGES

Every time they interpret contract, property, invested right ... they necessarily enact into laws part of a system of social philosophy.... The decisions of the courts on economic and social questions depend on their economic and social philosophy.

—Message to Congress,
December 8, 1908

The American people, and not the courts, are to determine their own fundamental policies. The people should have power to deal with the effects of acts of all their governmental agencies. This must be extended to include the effects of

JUDGES
[continued]

judicial acts as well as the acts of the executive and legislative representatives of the people.

> —Speech, National Convention of
> the Progressive Party, Chicago,
> Illinois, August 6, 1912

JUSTICE

Our constant aim is to do justice to every man, and to treat each man as by his own actions he shows that he deserves to be treated.

> —Oyster Bay, New York,
> August 18, 1906

The sons of all of us will pay in the future if we of the present do not do justice in the present.

> —Louisville, Kentucky, April 3, 1912

Our cause is the cause of justice for all in the interest of all.

> —Chicago, Illinois, June 17, 1912

LAW AND ORDER

The greatest benefit to the people, I am convinced, is the enforcement of the laws, without fear or favor.

—Speech to Friends of Honest Government, New York City, October 25, 1895

The substantial rights of the prisoner to a fair trial must of course be guaranteed ... but, subject to this guarantee, the law must work swiftly and surely and all the agents of the law should realize the wrong they do when they permit justice to be delayed or thwarted for technical or insufficient reasons.

—Letter to the governor of Indiana, August 6, 1903

No man is above the law and no man is below it; nor do we ask any man's permission when we require him to obey it.

—Third annual message to Congress, December 7, 1903

Obedience to the law is demanded as a right; not asked as a favor.

Ibid.

LAW AND ORDER
[continued]

Surely every one of us who knows his own heart must know that he too may stumble, and should be anxious to help his brother or sister who has stumbled. When the criminal has been punished, if he then shows a sincere desire to lead a decent and upright life, he should be given the chance, he should be helped and not hindered.

—*An Autobiography*, 1913

Order without liberty and liberty without order are equally destructive.
—*The Great Adventure*, 1918

LEADERSHIP

Unless a man believes in applied morality he is certain to be merely a noxious public servant.

—*The Outlook*, December 21, 1895

No man can lead a public career really worth leading, no man can act with rugged independence in serious crises, nor strike at great abuses, nor afford to make powerful and unscrupulous foes, if he is himself vulnerable in his private character.
—*An Autobiography*, 1913

There is always a tendency to believe that a hundred small men can furnish leadership equal to that of one big man. This is not so.

—*Ladies' Home Journal*, May 1917

The people can do nothing unless they have a man to get behind.

—Quoted in *Roosevelt, the Story of a Friendship*, Owen Wister, 1930

A stream cannot rise higher than its source.

Ibid.

LIBERTY

Throughout past history Liberty has always walked between the twin terrors of Tyranny and Anarchy. They have stalked like wolves beside her, with murder in their red eyes, ever-ready to tear each other's throats, but even more ready to render in sunder Liberty herself.

—*The Great Adventure*, 1911

LIFE

Life is not easy, and least of all is it easy for either the man or the nation that aspires to do great deeds.

—New York City, February 26, 1903

You often hear people speaking of life as if life was like striving upward toward a mountain peak. That is not so. Life is as if you were traveling a ridge crest. You have the gulf of inefficiency on one side and the gulf of wickedness on the other, and it helps not to have avoided one gulf if you fall into the other.

—The Groton School, Groton, Massachusetts, May 24, 1904

Life is a great adventure, and I want to say to you, accept it in such a spirit. I want to see you face it ready to do the best that lies in you to win out; and resolute, if you do not win out, to go down without complaining, doing the best that is in you, and abiding by the results.

—Address at Occidental College, Los Angeles, California, March 22, 1911

LIFE
[continued]

We cannot expect to escape a certain grayness in the afternoon of life—for it is not often that life ends in the splendor of a golden sunset.

—Quoted in *The Republican Roosevelt*,
John Morton Blum, 1954

LINCOLN

Lincoln is my hero. He was a man of the people who always felt with and for the people, but who had not the slightest touch of the demagogue in him.

—Letter to Sir George Otto
Trevelyan in England,
March 9, 1905

His unfaltering resolution, his quiet, unyielding courage, his infinite patience and gentleness, and the heights of disinterestedness which he attained whenever the crisis called for putting aside self, together with his far-sighted, hard-headed common sense point him out as just the kind of chief who do most good in a democratic republic like ours.

Ibid.

I never go into the White House and through the corridors and up the stairs … without thinking of old Lincoln … shambling, homely, with his strong, sad, deeply-furrowed face, all the time. I see him in the different rooms and in the halls.

—Quoted in *Theodore Roosevelt and His Times*, Joseph Bucklin Bishop, 1920

LITERATURE

In any great work of literature the first element is great imaginative power.

—*History as Literature*, 1913

THE LORD'S WORK

It is very essential that a man should have in him the capacity to defy his fellows if he thinks they are doing the work of the devil and not the work of the Lord; but it is even more essential for him to remember that he be most cautious about mistaking his own views for those of the Lord.

—*Oliver Cromwell*, 1900

THE LORD'S WORK
[continued]

We fight in honorable fashion for the good of mankind; fearless of the future; unheeding of our individual fates; with unflinching hearts and undimmed eyes; we stand at Armageddon, and we battle for the Lord.

—Chicago, Illinois, June 17, 1912

MARRIAGE

Throughout our history the success of the homemaker has been but another name for the up-building of the nation.

—Minnesota State Fair, St. Paul, September 2, 1901

The pangs of childbirth make all men debtors of all women.

—Letter, Oyster Bay, New York, July 19, 1903

Brutality by a man to a woman, by a grown person to a little child, by anything strong toward anything good and helpless, makes my blood literally boil. But I hate most of all the crime of a man against a woman.

Ibid.

A man must think well before he marries.

—An Autobiography, 1913

No words can paint the scorn and contempt which must be felt by all right-thinking men, not only for the brutal husband, but the husband who fails to show full loyalty and consideration for his wife. The partnership should be one of equal rights, one of love, of self-respect and unselfishness, above all a partnership for the performance of the most vitally important of all duties.

Ibid.

MINORITIES

Probably the best test of the true love of liberty in any country is the way in which minorities are treated in that country.

—Sorbonne, Paris, France,
April 23, 1910

MONEY

It is a false statement, and therefore it is a disservice to humanity, to say that money does not count. If a man had not got it he will find that it does count tremendously.

—Berkeley, California, 1911

MONEY
[continued]

No wise or generous soul will be content with a success which can be expressed only in dollars, but the soul which spurns all consideration of dollars usually drags down both itself and other souls into the gulf of the pitiful failure.

—*Ladies' Home Journal*, October 1916

MORAL STANDARDS

No prosperity and no glory can save a nation that is rotten at the heart.

—Minnesota State Fair, St. Paul,
September 2, 1901

There is not in all America a more dangerous trait than the deification of mere smartness unaccompanied by any sense of moral responsibility.

—Abilene, Kansas, May 2, 1903

It is a very bad thing to be morally callous, for moral callousness is a disease.

—Address to Harvard Union,
Harvard University,
Cambridge, Massachusetts,
February 23, 1907

The man who utters moral statements to which he does not try to live up, and the other man who listens and applauds the utterance of those sentiments and yet himself does not try to live up to them—both these men not only gain no good from what they have said and listened to, but have done themselves positive harm, because they have weakened just a little the spring of conscience within them.

Ibid.

MOTHERHOOD

Alone of human beings the good and wise mother stands on a plane of equal honor with the bravest soldier; for she has gladly gone down to the brink of the chasm of darkness to bring back the children in whose hands rests the future of the years.

—*The Great Adventure*, 1918

MUCKRAKING

Men with the muckrake are often indispensable to the well-being of society, but only if they know when to stop raking the muck.

—Washington, D.C., April 14, 1906

MUCKRAKING
[continued]

There should be relentless exposure of and attack upon
every evil practice, whether in politics, in business, or in social
life. I hail as a benefactor every writer or speaker, every man
who, on the platform, or in book, magazine or newspaper,
with merciless severity makes such attack, provided always that
he in his turn remembers that the attack is of use only if it is
absolutely truthful.

Ibid.

An epidemic of indiscriminate assault upon character does
not good, but very great harm.

Ibid.

NATIONAL DEFENSE

There is a homely adage which runs: "Speak softly and
carry a big stick; you will go far." If the American nation will
speak softly and yet build and keep at a pitch of the
highest training a thoroughly efficient navy, the Monroe
Doctrine will go far.

—*The Strenuous Life*, 1900

If we seek merely swollen, slothful ease and ignoble peace, if we shrink from the hard contests where men must win at the hazard of their lives and the risk of all they hold dear, then the bolder and stronger peoples will pass us by, and will win for themselves the domination of the world.

—Minnesota State Fair, St. Paul, September 2, 1901

NEW NATIONALISM

The New Nationalism puts the national need before sectional or personal advantage.

—Speech, "The New Nationalism," Osawatomie, Kansas, August 31, 1910, and published as *The New Nationalism*, 1910

I do not ask for overcentralization, but I do ask that we work in a spirit of broad and far-reaching nationalism when we work for what concerns our people as a whole.

Ibid.

NEW YORK

There is not a city on earth that deserves honest government more than New York, and no city in the Union lacks that kind of government more than our city.

—Speech to Friends of Honest
Government, New York City,
October 25, 1895

What is needed is common honesty, common sense, and common courage. We need the minor, the humdrum, the practical virtues—the commonplace virtues that are absolutely essential if we are to make this city what it should be. If these virtues are lacking, no amount of cleverness will answer.

> —Speech to Good Government Club, New York, April 15, 1897, on the occasion of his resignation as police commissioner

Any man who takes an active part in the varied, hurried, and interesting life of New York must be struck, not only by the number of the forces which tell for evil, but by the number of the forces which tell for good.

> —*McClure's Magazine*, 1901

NOBEL PEACE PRIZE

On being awarded the Nobel Peace Prize for his efforts to end the Russo-Japanese War, he wrote on December 5, 1906, to son Kermit:

I have been a little puzzled over the Nobel prize. It appears that there is a large sum of money—they say about $40,000.00—that goes with it. Now, I hate to do anything foolish or quixotic and above all I hate to do anything that means the refusal of money which would ultimately come to

NOBEL PEACE PRIZE
[continued]

you children. But [your mother] and I talked it over and came to the conclusion that while I was President at any rate, and perhaps anyhow, I could not accept money given to me for making peace between two nations, especially when I was able to make peace simply because I was President.

To receive money for making peace would in any event be a little too much like being given money for rescuing a man from drowning, or for performing a feat in war.

Ibid.

I am profoundly moved and touched by the signal honor shown me thru your body in conferring upon me the Nobel peace prize. There is no gift I could appreciate more; and I wish it were in my power to fully express my gratitude. I thank you for myself, and I thank you on behalf of the United States; for what I did I was able to accomplish only as representative of the Nation of which for the time being I am President. After much thought I have concluded that the best and most fitting way to apply the amount of the prize is by using it as a foundation to establish at Washington a permanent Industrial Peace Committee. The object will be to strive for better and more equitable relations among my countrymen who are engaged, whether as capitalists or wage-workers, in industrial and agricultural pursuits. This will carry out the purpose of the founder of the prize; for in modern life it is as important to work for the cause of just and righteous peace in the industrial

world as in the world of nations. I again express to you the
assurance of my deep and lasting gratitude and appreciation.

—Telegram to J. Lövland, Norwegian
minister for foreign affairs and
chairman of the Nobel Committee
of the Norwegian Parliament,
December 10, 1906

OPTIMISM

I am an optimist, but I hope I am a reasonably intelligent
one. I recognize that all the time there are numerous evil
forces at work, and that in places and at times they outweigh
the forces that tend for good. Hitherto, on the whole, the
good have come out ahead, and I think that they will in
the future.

—Letter to Owen Wister,
February 27, 1895

ORGANIZED LABOR

He who counsels violence does the cause of labor the
poorest service. Also, he loses the case.

—Speaking as New York police
commissioner to striking workers,
1895

ORGANIZED LABOR
[continued]

Labor organizations are like other organizations, like organizations of capitalists; sometimes they act very well and sometimes they act very badly. We should consistently favor them when they act well, and as fearlessly oppose them when they act badly.

—Berkeley, California,
March 23, 1911

It is essential that there should be organizations of labor. Capital organizes and therefore labor must organize.

—Milwaukee, Wisconsin,
October 14, 1912

PANAMA CANAL

The digging of the Panama Canal, the success with which it has been dug, has curiously enough, made a deeper impression abroad than at home.

—Harvard University, Cambridge,
Massachusetts,
December 14, 1910

It has been done with as near absolute cleanness, as near absolute honesty, as it is humanly possible to do any work, public or private.

Ibid.

PATRIOTISM

Patriotism means service to the nation; and only those who render such service are fit to enjoy the privilege of citizenship.

—Lincoln, Nebraska, June 14, 1917

The things that will destroy America are prosperity-at-any-price, peace-at-any-price, safety-first instead of duty first, the love of soft living and the get-rich-quick theory of life.

—Washington, D.C., January 1917,
*Proceedings of the Congress of
Constructive Patriotism*

PHILOSOPHY

Philosophy is a science just as history is a science. There is a need in one case as in the other for vivid and powerful pre-sentation of scientific matter in literary form.

—American Historical Association,
Boston, December 27, 1912

PLAY

I hope that soon all of our public schools will provide, in connection with the school buildings and during school hours, the place and time for recreation as well as study for children.

> —Letter to Cuno Hugo Rudolph, president of the Washington Playgrounds Association (which had opened the capital city's first playground in 1901), February 16, 1907

Play while you play and work while you work; and though play is a mighty good thing, remember that you had better never play at all than to get into a condition of mind where you regard play as the serious business of life, where you permit it to hamper and interfere with your doing your full duty in the real work of the world.

> —Address at Harvard Union, Harvard University, Cambridge, Massachusetts, February 23, 1907

Play should never be allowed to interfere with work; and a life devoted merely to play is, of all forms of existence, the most dismal.

> —*An Autobiography*, 1913

PLUCK

If a boy has not got pluck and honesty and common sense he is a pretty poor creature; and he is a worse creature if he is a man and lacks any one of those three traits.

—The Groton School, Groton,
Massachusetts, May 24, 1904

POLITICAL CAMPAIGN CONTRIBUTIONS

Let individuals contribute as they desire; but let us prohibit in effective fashion all corporations from making contributions for any political purpose, directly or indirectly.

—Sixth annual message to Congress,
December 3, 1906

POLITICS

I would rather go out of politics feeling that I had done what was right than stay in with the approval of all men, knowing in my heart that I had acted as I ought not to.

—Speech, New York Assembly, 1884

We must remember not to judge any public servant by any one act, and especially should we beware of attacking the men who are merely the occasions and not the causes of disaster.

—Hamilton Club, Chicago, Illinois,
April 10, 1899

POLITICS
[continued]

A lie is no more to be excused in politics than out
of politics.

—San Francisco, California,
May 14, 1903

It is a dreadful misfortune for a man to grow to feel that
his whole livelihood and whole happiness depend upon his
staying in office.

Ibid.

The most successful politician is he who says what everybody is thinking most often and in the loudest voice.

—Quoted in *Treasury of Humorous
Quotations*, Evan Esar, editor

POSTERITY

We are apt to speak of the judgment of "posterity" as
final; but "posterity" is no single entity, and the "posterity" of
one age has no necessary sympathy with the judgments of the
"posterity" that preceded it by a few centuries.

—*The Outlook*, April 30, 1910

POWER

Power invariably means both responsibility and danger.

—The White House, 1905

Power undirected by high purpose spells calamity, and high purpose by itself is utterly useless if the power to put it into effect is lacking.

—*The Outlook*, September 9, 1911

THE PRESIDENCY

Never, never, you must never remind a man at work on a political job that he may be President. It almost always kills him politically. He loses his nerve; he can't do his work; he gives up the very traits that are making him a possibility.

—To newspapermen Jacob A. Riis and Lincoln Steffens, New York Police Headquarters, November 1896

In midwinter or midsummer, with Congress sitting or absent, the President has always to be ready to devote every waking hour to some anxious, worrying, harassing matter, most difficult to decide, and yet which is imperative to immediately decide.

—*Youth's Companion*, November 6, 1902

THE PRESIDENCY
[continued]

One rather sad feature of the life of a President is the difficulty of making friends, because almost inevitably after a while the friend thinks there is some office he would like, applies for it, and when the President is obliged to refuse, feels that he has been injured.

Ibid.

What a place the Presidency is for learning to keep one's temper.

—Letter to son Kermit, June 17, 1906

Any man who has ever been honored by being made President of the United States is thereby forever after rendered the debtor of the American people, and is in honor bound throughout his life to remember this as his prime obligation; and in private life, as much as in public life, so to carry himself that the American people may never have cause to feel regret that once they placed him at their head.

—New York City, June 18, 1910

The presidency should be a powerful office, and the President a powerful man, who will take advantage of it; but as a corollary, a man who can be held accountable to the people, after a term of four years, and who will not occupy it for more than a stretch of eight years.

—Madison, Wisconsin, April 15, 1911

Editor's Note: TR ignored his own advice about not seeking a third term and was defeated when he tried; only after the death of TR's cousin, Franklin D. Roosevelt, did the people of the United States adopt a constitutional amendment limiting a president to two four-year terms.

When I left the presidency, I finished seven and a half years of administration, during which not one shot had been fired against a foreign foe. We were at absolute peace, and there was no nation in the world ... whom we had wronged, or from whom we had anything to fear.

—*An Autobiography*, 1913

There inheres in the Presidency more power than in any other office in any great republic or constitutional monarchy of modern times.

—Quoted in *The Republican Roosevelt*,
John Morton Blum, 1954

PRINCIPLES

Avoid the base hypocrisy of condemning in one man what you pass over in silence when committed by another.

—Cambridge, Massachusetts,
March 11, 1890

PRINCIPLES
[continued]

While I am in public life, however short a time that may be, I am in honor bound to act upon my beliefs and convictions. I do not intend to offend the prejudices of anyone else, but neither do I intend to allow their prejudices to make me false to my principles.

—Letter, November 8, 1901

PUBLIC SERVICE

There is no surer way of destroying the capacity for self-government in people than to accustom that people to demanding the impossible or the improper from its public men.

—San Francisco, California,
May 14, 1903

REFORM

A man who goes into politics should not expect to reform everything right off, with a jump.

—Buffalo, New York, July 26, 1893

When we undertake the impossible, we often fail to do anything at all.

—Chicago, Illinois,
September 3, 1900

More and more I have grown to have a horror of the reformer who is half charlatan and half fanatic, and ruins his own cause by overstatement.

—Oyster Bay, New York,
July 20, 1901

REFORM
[continued]

People who call themselves anarchists, no matter how they qualify the word by calling themselves "reformers," by just so much add to the strength of our worst and most vicious elements of our civilization.

—Letter to Owen Wister,
November 10, 1908

We know that there are in life injustices which we are powerless to remedy. But we also know that there is much injustice which can be remedied.

—*The Outlook*, March 27, 1909

The long path leading upward toward the light cannot be traversed at once, or in a day, or in a year. But there are certain steps that can be taken.... Having taken these first steps, we shall see more clearly how to walk still further with a bolder stride.

—New York, October 30, 1912

It is one thing to listen in perfunctory fashion to tales of overcrowded tenements, and it is quite another actually to see what the overcrowding means, some hot summer night, by even a single inspection during the hours of darkness.

—*An Autobiography*, 1913

RELIGION

You are not going to make any new commandments at this stage which will supply the place of the old ones. The truths that were true at the foot of Mt. Sinai are true now.

—Oyster Bay, New York,
September 8, 1906

The man who preaches decency and straight dealing occupies a peculiarly contemptible position if he does not try himself to practice what he preaches.

Ibid.

No man is a good citizen unless he so acts as to show that he actually uses the Ten Commandments, and translates the Golden Rule into his life conduct.

—Boy Scouts of America handbook,
1911

A churchless community, a community where men have abandoned and scoffed at or ignored their religious needs, is a community on the rapid down grade.

—*Ladies' Home Journal*,
December 1916

RELIGION
[continued]

On Sunday, go to church. Yes—I know all the excuses. I know that one can worship the Creator and dedicate oneself to good living in a grove of trees, or by a running brook, or in one's own house, just as well as in church. But I also know that as a matter of cold fact the average man does not thus worship or thus dedicate himself. If he stays away from church he does not spend his time in good works or lofty meditation. He looks over the colored supplement of the newspaper; he yawns; and he finally seeks relief from the mental vacuity of isolation by going where the combined mental vacuity of many partially relieves the mental vacuity of each particular individual.

—*Ladies' Home Journal*, October 1917

RIDING

Any man, if he chooses, can gradually school himself to the requisite nerve [to ride], and gradually learn the requisite seat and hands, that will enable him to do respectably across country, or to perform the average work on a ranch.

—*An Autobiography*, 1913

SELF-RELIANCE AND SELF-RESPECT

It is both foolish and wicked to teach the average man who is not well off that some wrong or injustice has been done him, and that he should hope for redress elsewhere than in his own industry, honesty and intelligence.

—*Review of Reviews*, January 1897

The worst lesson that can be taught to a man is to rely upon others and to whine over his sufferings.

Ibid.

If an American is to amount to anything he must rely upon himself, and not upon the State; he must take pride in his own work, instead of sitting idle to envy the luck of others; he must face life with resolute courage, win victory if he can, and accept defeat if he must, without seeking to place on his fellow man a responsibility which is not theirs.

Ibid.

SHOOTING

There are men whose eye and hand are so quick and so sure they achieve a perfection of marksmanship to which no practice will enable ordinary men to attain. There are other

SHOOTING
[continued]

men who cannot learn to shoot with any accuracy at all. In between come the mass of men of ordinary abilities, who, if they choose resolutely to practice, can by sheer industry and judgment make themselves fair rifle shots.

—*An Autobiography*, 1913

SIMPLIFIED SPELLING

For a brief time TR embraced a movement to alter spelling of certain words, such as through *to* thru *(as you will have noticed in some of TR's spellings in quotations in this book) and* dropped *to* dropt. *The movement was led by the Simplified Spelling Board, located in New York City. TR's role in this movement was to issue an executive order requiring all the publications of federal executive departments to conform to the board's guidelines.*

There is not the slightest intention to do anything revolutionary or initiate any far-reaching policy. The purpose simply is for the Government, instead of lagging behind popular sentiment, to advance abreast of it and at the same time abreast of the views of the ablest and most practical educators of our time as well as the most profound scholars.

—Oyster Bay, New York,
August 27, 1906

If the slight changes in the spelling of the three hundred words proposed wholly or partially meet popular approval, then the changes will become permanent without any reference to what public officials or individual private citizens may feel; if they do not ultimately meet with popular approval they will be dropt, and that is all there is about it.

Ibid.

It is not an attack on the language of Shakespeare and Milton.

Ibid.

I firmly believe that the great majority of the changes that I have authorized will by the middle of the present century be regular, ordinary, commonplace English.

—Oyster Bay, New York,
September 11, 1906

If I know that element in Boston which already regards me as dangerous, its worst fears will have been realized by my action about spelling.

—Letter, Oyster Bay, New York,
September 13, 1906

Acknowledging defeat on the spelling issue, but unwilling to go back to the old spelling, TR wrote to a friend on December 16, 1906:
I could not by fighting have kept the new spelling in, and it was evidently worse than useless to go into an undignified

SIMPLIFIED SPELLING
[continued]

contest when I was beaten. Do you know I think that the one word as to which I thought the new spelling was wrong—thru—was more responsible for our discomfiture? But I am mighty glad that I did the thing anyhow. In my own correspondence I shall continue using the new spelling.

SPORTS

The years of late boyhood and early manhood—say from twelve or fourteen to twenty-eight or thirty, and often much later—are those in which athletic sports prove not only most attractive, but also most beneficial to the individual.... In college—and in most of the schools which are preparatory for college—rowing, football, baseball, running, jumping, sparring, and the like have assumed a constantly increasing prominence.

—*North American Review*,
August 1890

Athletic sports, if followed properly, and not elevated into a fetish, are admirable for developing character, besides bestowing on participants an invaluable fund of health and strength.

Ibid.

It is a good thing for a boy to have captained his school or college eleven, but it is a very bad thing if, twenty years afterward, all that can be said of him is that he has continued to take an interest in football, baseball, or boxing, and has with him the memory that he was once captain.

—"Character and Success,"
The Outlook, March 31, 1900

Athletics are good; study is even better; and best of all is the development of the type of character for the lack of which, in an individual as in a nation, no amount of brilliancy of mind or strength of body will atone.

—Address to Harvard Union,
Harvard University,
Cambridge, Massachusetts,
February 23, 1907

THE SQUARE DEAL

We must treat each man on his worth and merits as a man. We must see that each is given a square deal, because he is entitled to no more and should receive no less.

—New York State Fair, Syracuse,
September 7, 1903

THE SQUARE DEAL
[continued]

When I say I am for the square deal I mean not merely that I stand for fair play under the present rules of the game, but that I stand for having those rules changed so as to work for a more substantial equality of opportunity and of reward for equally good service.

—Osawatomie, Kansas,
August 31, 1910

A square deal for every man! That is the only safe motto for the United States.
—Letter, July 17, 1917

SUCCESS

Success—the real success—does not depend upon the position you hold, but upon how you carry yourself in that position.
—University of Cambridge, England,
May 26, 1910

Nothing in the world is worth having or worth doing unless it means effort, pain, difficulty … I have never in my life envied a human being who led an easy life; I have envied a great many people who led difficult lives and led them well.

—Des Moines, Iowa,
November 4, 1910

SUCCESS

[continued]

I have never won anything without hard labor and the exercise of my best judgment and careful planning and working long in advance.

Ibid.

TAXES

Absolute equality, absolute justice in matters of taxation will probably never be realized.

—Message to New York Legislature,
January 3, 1900

THE TRUE CHRISTIAN

The true Christian is the true citizen, lofty of purpose, resolute in endeavor, ready for a hero's deeds, but never looking down on his task because it is cast in the day of small things; scornful of baseness, awake to his own duties as well as to his rights, following the higher law with reverence, and in this world doing all that in him lies, so that when death comes

he may feel that mankind is in some degree better because he
has lived.

—Speech to Young Men's Christian
Association of New York City,
March 1901

TRUTH IN LABELING

The Pure Food Law is largely a labeling law, and
"misbranding" is to use a false or deceptive label—that is,
one deceptive to the average consumer.

—The White House, March 16, 1907

*A complaint by Thomas E. Wilson, Chicago meatpacker and
founder of Wilson and Company, drew this response by way of a letter from TR to James Wilson (no relation), Secretary of
Agriculture:*

Mr. Wilson's ... complaint is of being required to leave off
the word "Bologna" from sausages, on the ground that it is not
made in Bologna. I think on this he is right. Bologna sausages are not commonly understood to be made in Bologna any
more than Castile soap is understood to be made in Spain. It
would be nonsense to refuse to allow a person to use the term
"Castile" unless the soap was made in Spain. So it would seem
to me to be nonsense to refuse to allow people to use the word

TRUTH IN LABELING
[continued]

"Bologna" before "sausage" if, as a matter of fact, it is the same sausage as people call Bologna sausage. Not one in a thousand persons knows where Bologna is—and I personally am not that one.

—Oyster Bay, New York,
September 12, 1906

In a letter to the secretary of agriculture, in which TR kept his pledge to continue using Simplified Spelling, he sought to clarify the labeling of whiskies:

It appears that two or more whiskies are sometimes mixt together and the mixture sold as a blended whisky. There is no question, therefore, that the label "blended whisky" should apply to such a mixture. There ought to be some way of informing the consumer whether he is furnished a mixture of two whiskies, or of whisky and neutral spirit or grain distillate.... If the average consumer receives a mixture of whisky and neutral spirit labeled "blended whisky," he will naturally conclude that two or more whiskies of different ages or distillations have been added together.... Taking all these considerations together it seems to me that only a mixture of whiskies should be labeled "blended whisky."

—The White House, March 16, 1907

TURNING SIXTY

I am glad to be sixty, for it somehow gives me the right to be titularly as old as I feel. I only hope that when you are sixty you'll have had as much happiness to look back upon as I have had.

—Letter to son Kermit,
October 17, 1918

VETERANS

A man who is good enough to shed his blood for his country is good enough to be given a square deal afterwards. More than that no man is entitled, and less than that no man shall have.

—Speech, Springfield, Illinois,
July 4, 1903

THE VICE-PRESIDENCY

The presidency being all important, and the vice-presidency of comparatively little note, the entire strength of the contending factions is spent in the conflict over the first, and very often a man who is most anxious to take the first

THE VICE-PRESIDENCY
[continued]

place will not take the second, preferring some other political position. It has thus frequently happened that the two candidates have been totally dissimilar in character and even in party principle, though both running on the same ticket. Very odd results have followed in more than one instance.

—*Review of Reviews*, September 1896

He should always be a man who would be consulted by the President on every great party issue. It would be very well if he were given a seat in the Cabinet.

Ibid.

I have been vice-president, and know how hollow the honor is.

—Quoted in *Impressions of Theodore Roosevelt*, Lawrence F. Abbott, 1922

VIRTUE

The corrupt men have been perfectly content to let their opponents monopolize all the virtue while they themselves have been permitted to monopolize all the efficiency.

—*The Outlook*, December 21, 1895

VIRTUE

[continued]

To sit home, read one's favorite paper, and scoff at the misdeeds of the men who do things is easy, but it is markedly ineffective. It is what evil men count upon the good men's doing.

Ibid.

The virtue that is worth having is the virtue that can sustain the rough shock of actual living, the virtue that can achieve practical results, that finds expression in actual life.

—New York, New York,
January 18, 1899

VOTING

A vote is like a rifle: its usefulness depends upon the character of the user.

—*An Autobiography*, 1913

WAR AND PEACE

A nation should never fight unless forced to; but it should always be ready to fight.

—U.S. Naval War College, Newport,
Rhode Island, June 2, 1897

No qualities called out by a purely peaceful life stand to a level with those stern and virile virtues which move the men of stout heart and strong hand who uphold the honor of their flag in battle.

—*The Bookman*, June 1897

I abhor unjust war.

—*An Autobiography*, 1913

I respect all men and women who from high motives and with sanity and self-respect do all they can to avert war.

Ibid.

Our people are not military.

Ibid.

I advocate preparation for war in order to avert war; and I should never advocate war unless it were the only alternative to dishonor.

Ibid.

All men who feel any power of joy in battle know what it is like when the wolf rises in the heart.

—*Works of Theodore Roosevelt*,
edited by Hermann Hagedorn,
1926

WEALTH

The acquisition of wealth is not in the least the only test of success. After a certain amount of wealth has been accumulated, the accumulation of more is of very little consequence indeed from the standpoint of success, as success should be understood both by the community and the individual.

—"Character and Success,"
The Outlook, March 31, 1900

I am far from underestimating the importance of dividends; but I rank dividends below human character.

—*The New Nationalism*, 1910

Of all forms of tyranny the least attractive and the most vulgar is the tyranny of mere wealth.

—Provincetown, Massachusetts,
August 20, 1907

THE WEST

I would strongly recommend some of our gilded youth to go West and try a short course of riding bucking ponies, and assist at the branding of a lot of Texas steers.

—New York *Tribune*, July 18, 1884

I owe more than I ever can express to the West, which of
course means to the men and women I met in the West.

—*An Autobiography*, 1913

THE WEST
[continued]

We had a free and hardy life with horse and rifle. We worked under the scorching midsummer sun, when the wide plains shimmered and wavered in the heat, and we knew the freezing misery of riding night guard around the cattle in the late fall roundup. In the soft springtime the stars were glorious in our eyes, each night before we fell asleep; and in the winter we rode through blinding blizzards, when the driven snowdust burned our faces. There were monotonous days, as we guided the trail cattle, or the beef herds, hour after hour at the slowest of walks; and minutes or hours teeming with excitement as we stopped stampedes or swam the herds across rivers treacherous with quicksand, or brimmed with running ice. We knew toil and hardship and hunger and thirst; and we saw men die, violent deaths as they worked among the horses and cattle, or fought in evil feuds with one another, but we felt the beat of hardy life in our veins, and ours was the glory of work and the joy of living.

—*An Autobiography*, 1913

Nowhere, not even at sea, does a man feel more lonely than when riding over the far-reaching, seemingly never-ending plains … their vastness and loneliness and their monotony have a strong fascination for him.

—*Works of Theodore Roosevelt*,
edited by Hermann Hagedorn,
1926

WHISKEY

I [carried] a flask of whisky [on hunting expeditions] for emergencies—although, as I found out that tea was better than whisky when a man was cold or done out, I abandoned the practice of taking whisky on hunting trips.

—*An Autobiography*, 1913

THE WHITE HOUSE

In 1902 the "President's House" was officially renamed "the White House" by executive order. The presidential residence was also extensively renovated, including carrying out massive repairs to its electrical wiring and utilities and moving offices from the second floor to an executive suite of offices in a new addition known as the West Wing. Of the work of the architectural firm of McKim, Mead, and White, TR said:

The changes in the White House have transformed it from a shabby likeness to the ground floor of the Astor House into a simple and dignified dwelling for the head of a great republic.

—Quoted in *Theodore Roosevelt: A Life*, Nathan Miller, 1992

THE WHITE HOUSE
[continued]

I don't think any President ever enjoyed himself more than I did. Moreover, I don't think any ex-President ever enjoyed himself more.

—University of Cambridge, England,
May 26, 1910

While President, I have *been* President, emphatically; I have used every ounce of power there was in the office and I have not cared a rap for the criticisms of those who spoke of "usurpation of power"; for I knew that the talk was all nonsense and that there was no usurpation.... I have felt not merely that my action was right in itself, but that in showing the strength of, or in giving strength to the executive, I was establishing a precedent of value. I believe in a strong executive; I believe in power; but I believe that the strong executive should be a perpetual executive.

—Quoted in *The American Presidents*,
David C. Whitney, 1975

WINNING

No triumph of peace is quite so great as the supreme triumphs of war.

—Speech at U.S. Naval War College,
Newport, Rhode Island,
June 2, 1897

It is more difficult to preserve the fruits of victory than to win the victory.

—*McClure's Magazine*, October 1901

WISDOM

The wisdom of one generation may seem the folly of the next.

—*History as Literature*, 1913

WOMEN'S RIGHTS

Viewed purely in the abstract, I think there can be no question that women should have equal rights with men.

—Senior thesis at Harvard, "The Practicability of Equalizing Men and Women before the Law," 1880

Especially as regards the laws relating to marraige [sic] there should be the most absolute equality between the two sexes. *I do not think the woman should assume the man's name.*

Ibid.

WOMEN'S RIGHTS
[continued]

Working women have the same need to [the same] protection that working men have; the ballot is as necessary for one class as to the other; we do not believe that with the two sexes there is identity of function; but we do believe there should be equality of right.

> —Speech, National Convention of
> the Progressive Party, Chicago,
> Illinois, August 6, 1912

Much can be done by law towards putting women on a footing of complete and entire equal rights with man—including the right to vote, the right to hold and use property, and the right to enter any profession she desires on the same terms as the man.

> —*An Autobiography*, 1913

Women should have free access to every field of labor which they care to enter, and when their work is as valuable as that of a man it should be paid as highly.

> Ibid.

WORDS

I have a perfect horror of words that are not backed up by deeds.

—Oyster Bay, New York, July 7, 1915

One of our defects as a nation is a tendency to use what have been called "weasel words." When a weasel sucks eggs the meat is sucked out of the egg. If you use a "weasel word" after another there is nothing left of the other.

—St. Louis, Missouri, May 31, 1916

WORK

The law of worthy work well done is the law of successful American life.

—Chattanooga, Tennessee,
November 4, 1903

WRESTLING

I have had to abandon wrestling because I found that in such violent work I tended to lay myself up; and I do but little boxing because it seems rather absurd for a President to appear with a black eye or a swollen nose or a cut lip.

—Letter, June 15, 1903

WRESTLING
[continued]

I am wrestling with two Japanese wrestlers three times a week. I am not the age or build one would think to be whirled lightly over an opponent's head and batted down on a mattress without damage. But they are so skillful that I have not been hurt at all. My throat is a little sore, because once when one of them had a strangle hold I also got hold of his windpipe and thought I could perhaps choke him off before he could choke me. However, he got ahead.

—Letter to son Kermit, April 9, 1904

When TR was governor of New York he was visited in Albany by the champion middleweight wrestler of America. The two wrestled two or three times a week for a couple of months. When the professional left the city, TR's opponent was a local professional rower, who knew about boats and oars but little about wrestling:

By the end of our second afternoon one of his long ribs had been caved in, and my left shoulder so nearly shoved out of place that it creaked. He was nearly as pleased as I was when I told him that I thought we would "vote the war a failure" and abandon wrestling.

—An Autobiography, 1913

Wrestling is a much more violent amusement than boxing.

—An Autobiography, 1913

YOSEMITE PARK

After touring California's Yosemite Park with naturalist John Muir, TR described spending a night on a bed of fir boughs under limbs of giant sequoia trees, listening to the evensong of the Rocky Mountain hermit thrush and the roar of the park's titanic waterfalls:

It was like lying in a great solemn cathedral, far vaster and more beautiful than any built by the hand of man.

—Quoted in *Theodore Roosevelt,*
Strenuous American,
Alvin F. Harlow, 1934

TR's Last Words

*In poor health and grieving the death of his youngest son,
Quentin, in aerial combat in World War I, TR was in bed near
mid-night, January 5, 1919. Having just written a memo on the
subject of averting a split among Senate and House Republicans on
domestic policies, he turned to his valet, James Amos, a black man
who had been with him since his White House days, and spoke his
last words:*

Please put out that light, James.

The Arena

In an address at the Sorbonne in Paris, France, on April 23, 1910, TR provided what students of his life and career have come to consider the perfect summation of his personal and political philosophy. Although TR is frequently quoted in part or in essence, most often by politicians and athletes, the only national figure to cite TR verbatim and from memory was President Richard M. Nixon during his farewell remarks in the East Room of the White House on the morning of his resignation from the presidency in 1974.

It is not the critic who counts, not the man who points out how the strong man stumbled or where the doer of deeds could have done better. The credit belongs to the man who is actually in the arena; whose face is marred by dust and sweat and blood; who errs and comes short again … who knows the great enthusiasms, the great devotions, and spends himself in a worthy cause; who at least knows in the end the triumph of high achievement; and who, at worst, if he fails, at least fails while doing greatly, so that his place shall never be with those cold and timid souls who know neither victory nor defeat.

Roosevelt on the Rough Riders

From George Washington to George Bush, men who had gone to war before becoming president of the United States had done so reluctantly and with revulsion. But in 1898, Theodore Roosevelt not only encouraged his countrymen to go to war to wrest Cuba from Spain, he also volunteered to organize a regiment of cavalry to fight in it, with himself as its leader. "He was so overflowing with patriotism," said a friend, "that he could not restrain himself."

The name popularized by newspapers for Roosevelt's regiment was "Rough Riders." This did not please TR at first. He explained at a press conference in Washington on April 28, 1898: "The objection to that term is that people who read it may get the impression that the regiment is a hippodrome affair. Those who get that idea will discover that it is a mistake. The regiment may be one of rough riders, but they will be as orderly, obedient, and generally well disciplined a body as any equal number of men in any branch of the service. But they will not make a show. They go out for business, and when they do business no one will entertain for a moment that they are part of a show."

Members of the regiment were drawn from gentlemen horsemen from the East, polo players, athletes, adventuresome youths from well-to-do families, and, by far the greatest numbers, out of the wild and woolly West. Even TR agreed that history had never seen anything like them. He wrote to his longtime friend and political mentor, Senator Henry Cabot Lodge, "Three fourths of our men have at one time or another been cowboys.... They are intelligent as well as game."

Eager to lead them into battle and, perhaps, to glory, TR sent the following telegram to Brooks Brothers in New York, ordering uniforms:

Washington, D.C., May 2, 1898

Ordinary cavalry lieutenant colonel's uniform in blue Cravenette.

Heading to the training ground at San Antonio, Texas, to join and lead the regiment, TR wrote to sister Corinne Roosevelt Robinson on May 5, 1898:

I feel rather like a fake at going; for we may never get down to Cuba and if we do I don't think we shall see any serious campaigning.

Blessed Bunnies, It has been a real holiday to have darling mother here. Yesterday I brought her out to the camp, and she saw it all—the men, the tents in the long company streets, the horses being taken to water, my little horse Texas, the colonel and all the majors, and finally the [mascots] mountain lion and the jolly little dog Cuba, who had several fights while she looked on. The mountain lion is not much more than a kitten as yet, but it is very cross and treacherous.

> —Letter to his children concerning
> the visit of Edith Roosevelt to the
> Rough Riders embarkation camp,
> Tampa, Florida, June 6, 1898

THE ROUGH RIDERS
[continued]

If our hopes are realized we sail tomorrow for Cuba, but nobody can tell how many of us will get back, and I don't suppose there is much glory ahead, but I hope and believe we shall do our duty, and the homecoming will be very pleasant for those that do get home.

—Letter to sister Corinne, Tampa,
June 7, 1898

We have a lovely camp here, by a beautiful stream which runs through jungle-lined banks. So far the country is lovely; plenty of grass and great open woods of palms.

—Letter to sister Anna Roosevelt
Cowles, five miles from Santiago de
Cuba, June 27, 1898

The morning after the fight [at Las Guasimas] we buried our dead in a great big trench, reading the solemn burial service over them, and all the regiment joining in singing "Rock of Ages." The vultures were wheeling overhead by hundreds.

Ibid.

COL. THED. ROOSEVELT.

THE ROUGH RIDERS
[continued]

Whatever comes I shall feel contented with having left the Navy Department to go into the army for the war, for our regiment has been in the first fight on land, and has done well.

—Letter to Henry Cabot Lodge,
June 27, 1898

The battle simply fought itself.

—To General Leonard Wood
following the charge up
San Juan Hill, July 4, 1898

The fighting has been very hard. I don't know whether people at home know how well this regiment did. I am as proud of it as I can be; and these men would follow me anywhere now. It was great luck for me to get command of it before this battle.

—Letter to Henry Cabot Lodge,
July 5, 1898

I have led this regiment during the last three weeks—the crowning weeks of my life.

—To brother-in-law Douglas
Robinson, July 19, 1898

I have not yet had time to wonder what I shall do when I get out of this.

Ibid.

"Triumph tasted"—for that one will readily pay as heavy a price as we have paid.

—Letter to Corinne Roosevelt
Robinson, July 19, 1898

The only way to get them [the Rough Riders] to do it in the way it had to be done was to lead them myself.

Ibid.

Somehow or other I always knew that if I did not go I never would forgive myself; and I really have been of use.

—Letter to Henry Cabot Lodge,
July 19, 1898

We had a bully fight at Santiago, and though there was an immense amount that I did not exactly enjoy, the charge itself was great fun.

—Letter to Douglas Robinson,
July 27, 1898

THE ROUGH RIDERS
[continued]

I would rather have led that charge and earned my colonelcy than served three terms in the United States Senate. It makes me feel as though I could now leave something to my children which will serve as an apology for my having existed.

Ibid.

The good people of New York seem to be crazy over me; it is not very long since on the whole they felt I compared unfavorably with Caligula.

—Letter to Henry Cabot Lodge,
Santiago, Cuba, July 31, 1898

We had a great time and this is a regiment of cracker-jacks—American from start to finish, in the best and fullest sense of the term.

—Aboard ship heading for home,
August 14, 1898

Don't any of you get gay and pose as heroes. Don't go back and lie on your laurels. They will wither.

—To the Rough Riders at their
mustering-out ceremony,
Montauk, Long Island, New York,
September 15, 1898

We were all in the spirit of the thing and greatly excited by the charge, the men cheering and running forward between shots.

—*The Rough Riders*, 1899

I waved my hat, and we went up the hill in a rush.

—*An Autobiography*, 1913

Here's all this fuss now about the Rough Riders and me. I've reached the crest of the wave. Now I'll probably begin to go down.

—September 1898, quoted in *The Roosevelt Family of Sagamore Hill*, Hermann Hagedorn, 1934

Quotations about Theodore Roosevelt

When the Rough Riders returned from their triumph in Cuba to be hailed as heroes, their leader was described by one newspaper as the most famous man in America. But adjectives were nothing new to TR. Since his political debut in the New York State Assembly in 1880, he had been a handy lightning rod for a series of journalistic thunderbolts. These were frequently complimentary, although sometimes begrudgingly so. But few men in public life before or since felt the sting of criticism in so personal a manner. This was demonstrated in the Philadelphia North American on October 10, 1912. Four days before TR was shot in Milwaukee the paper published a list of epithets that had been applied to him in another publication in a single month:

> *Shrieks his hostility, ridiculous, contemptible, eager to use fraud, unparalleled viciousness and dishonesty, insensate ambition, gnashing his teeth, dangerous demagogue, charlatan, plain aberration, bad faith, unworthy methods, dangerous, shocking, unscrupulous, horrible glibness, indecent performance, an Aaron Burr, shameless, crazy socialistic schemer, blatantly insincere, hypocritical, in favor of howling mobocracy, user of shabby tactics, hollow and untrustworthy, duplicitous, shrewd political trickster, a self-seeking autocrat, guilty of a squalid bandying of words, no respecter of truth, and full of unblushing effrontery.*

Although TR had felt the scorn of countless publications, only one felt the Roosevelt wrath in the form of a libel suit. In October 1912, the weekly Michigan paper Iron Ore accused him of political and personal blackguardism but then went on to say, "He gets drunk, too, and that not infrequently, and all his intimates know about it."

If people close to TR knew anything about him, it was that he was not a drunkard. He enjoyed a glass of wine with a meal, they said (and TR admitted), but he didn't like and didn't drink beer or whiskey. Friends and political associates flocked into court to testify on his behalf. The newspaper publisher, unable to prove his allegations, withdrew them in court, saying he had based his allegations on "gossip." Because Roosevelt had informed the court that he sought no financial damages, but merely wanted his reputation secured, the judge ordered the jury to find in Roosevelt's favor and awarded him what TR had asked: "nominal damages." Under Michigan law, that came to six cents.

Here is a sampling of things that were said about Roosevelt over the course of his career in politics.

The young gentleman has been dubbed "Oscar Wilde" by admiring colleagues, who were much amused by his elastic movements and wealth of mouth.

> —Newspaper report of TR's first
> speech in the New York State
> Assembly, January 1881

QUOTATIONS ABOUT THEODORE ROOSEVELT
[continued]

The man is a joke, a dude.

> —New York State Assemblyman
> Isaac J. Hunt on the fancy attire
> TR wore on his first day as an
> assemblyman, January 1881

Ten years from now, he will still be a young man for the Governor's chair, or a seat in the United States Senate, and there are experienced politicians who believe the Presidency itself lies in the path of the man.

> —*Washington Star*, on TR leaving the
> Civil Service Commission in
> Washington, D.C., to become
> police commissioner in New York,
> April 1895

We have a real police commissioner. His name is Theodore Roosevelt. His teeth are big and white, his eyes are small and piercing, his voice is rasping. When he asks a question, Mr. Roosevelt shoots at the poor trembling policeman as he would shoot a bullet at a coyote. He shows a set of teeth calculated to unnerve the bravest of the Finest. His teeth are very white and almost as big as a colt's. They are broad teeth, they form a perfectly straight line. The lower teeth look like a row of dominoes. They do not lap over or under each other, as most teeth do, but come together evenly. They seem to say, "Tell the truth to your commissioner, or he'll bite your head off."

Generally speaking, this interesting Commissioner's face is red. He has lived a great deal out of doors, and that accounts for it. His hair is thick and short. Under his right ear he has a long scar. It is the opinion of all the policemen who have talked to him that he got the scar fighting an Indian out West. It is also their opinion that the Indian is dead.

But Mr. Roosevelt's voice is the policeman's hardest trial. It is an exasperating voice, a sharp voice, a rasping voice. It is a voice that comes from the tips of the teeth and seems to say in its tones, "What do you amount to, anyway?"

One thing our noble force may make its mind up to at once—it must do as Roosevelt says, for it is not likely that it will succeed in beating him.

—*New York World*, May 16, 1895

You are rushing so rapidly to the front that that day is not far distant when you will come into a larger kingdom.

—Letter from Henry Cabot Lodge,
August 1895

The service he has rendered the city is second to that of none, and considering the conditions surrounding it, it is in our judgment unequaled.

—Editorial concerning TR's
resignation as head of the police
board, *New York Times*, March 1897

QUOTATIONS ABOUT THEODORE ROOSEVELT

[continued]

I have a concern to put on record my earnest belief that in New York you are doing the greatest work of which any American today is capable, and exhibiting to the young men of the country the spectacle of a very important office administered by a man of high character in the most efficient way amid a thousand difficulties. I cannot think of anything more instructive.

> —Letter from E. L. Godkin, editor of the *Evening Post* and frequent critic of TR, March 1897

The liveliest spot in Washington at present is the Navy Department. The decks are cleared for action. Acting Secretary Roosevelt has the whole Navy bordering on a war footing. It remains only to sand down decks and pipe to quarters for action.

> —*New York Sun*, August 23, 1897

If he becomes Governor of New York, sooner or later, with his personality, he will have to be President of the United States.

> —New York State Republican boss Thomas Platt, September 3, 1898

His plain performance of a plain duty, the doing right because it was right, taught us a lesson we stood in greater need of than of any other. Roosevelt's campaign for reform of the police force became the moral issue of the day. It swept the cobwebs out of our civic brains, and blew the dust from our eyes, so that we saw clearly where all had been confusion before: saw straight, rather. We rarely realize, in these latter days, how much of our ability to fight for good government, and our hope of winning the fight, is due to the campaign of honesty waged by Theodore Roosevelt in Mulberry Street.

—Jacob A. Riis, *Theodore Roosevelt the Citizen*, 1903

I have not seen much of Mr. Roosevelt since he became President, but I am told that he sooner thinks than he talks, which is a miracle not wholly in accord with the educational theory of forming an opinion.

—Woodrow Wilson, November 1907

He is essentially a fighter and when he gets into a fight he is completely dominated by the desire to destroy his adversary. He instinctively lays hold of every weapon which can be used for that end ... as one might pick up a poker or chair with which to strike.

—Republican Party leader Elihu Root, March 9, 1912

QUOTATIONS ABOUT THEODORE ROOSEVELT
[continued]

Like all Americans I had a sympathy for his irresistible energy and courage.... In practically every field of human endeavor he has made his mark.

> —Letter from Newton B. Baker to General John J. Pershing on the death of TR, January 6, 1919

So Valiant-for-Truth passed over and all the trumpets sounded for him on the other side.

> —Henry Cabot Lodge, speech to the U.S. Senate, January 6, 1919

That Theodore is in earnest and sincere, there is no room for doubt in my mind. People who hate him ... credit him neither with sincerity nor honesty.... At the same time it is to be remembered that he has a reputation of being the most far-sighted politician in the country.

> —Letter from a TR friend, Robert Grant, March 1912, quoted in *Power and Responsibility*, William Henry Harbaugh, 1961

By his words and deeds he gave a defining and supporting frame for the aspirations of those insufficiently clear or strong to support their aspirations by their own endeavor. Men, in the hope of finding their better selves, attached themselves to him.

—Elting E. Morison, editor, *The Letters of Theodore Roosevelt*, 8 vols., 1951–1954, quoted in *Power and Responsibility*, William Henry Harbaugh, 1961

You had to hate the Colonel a whole lot to keep from loving him.

—Newspaperman Irvin S. Cobb, quoted in *Power and Responsibility*, William Henry Harbaugh, 1961

Theodore Roosevelt Chronology

1858	Born, October 27 at 28 East 20th Street, New York City.
1880	Graduates from Harvard University, begins study of law at Columbia University, joins Republican Party, marries Alice Lee.
1881–1884	Member, New York State Legislature. Publishes first book, *The Naval War of 1812* (1881). First hunting trip to Dakota, invests in cattle (1883).
1884	Birth of daughter Alice. Deaths of his wife and mother on same day. Delegate to Republican National Convention.
1884–1886	Ranching in Dakota, publishes *Hunting Trips of a Ranchman* (1885).
1886	Defeated in election for mayor of New York. Publishes biography of Thomas Hart Benton. Marries Edith Kermit Carow in London.
1887	First son, Theodore, Jr., born.
1887–1888	Publishes three books.
1889	Second son, Kermit, born.
1889–1895	Member, U.S. Civil Service Commission, residing with family in Washington, D.C. Publishes four-volume *The Winning of the West*. Second daughter, Ethel, born (1891); third son, Archibald, born (1894).

1895–1897	President, Police Board of Commissioners, New York City. Garners national press attention for "midnight rambles" during which he catches slacking policemen.
1897–1898	Assistant secretary of the navy; son Quentin born, November 19, 1897; TR agitates for U.S. liberation of Cuba from Spain and vows to join the fight as cavalryman. Organizes the "Rough Riders," leads them in victorious charge to capture the San Juan heights overlooking Santiago de Cuba. Hailed as hero, proposed for (but denied) Congressional Medal of Honor.
1898	Elected governor of New York.
1899	Publishes war memoir, *The Rough Riders*.
1900	Elected vice president. Publishes *Oliver Cromwell*.
1901	President William McKinley dies September 14, after being shot, thrusting TR into the presidency at age forty-six.
1901–1909	President of the United States. Fosters a revolution against Colombia, resulting in independence for Panama, clearing the way for building the Panama Canal. Wages campaign against industrial trusts. In 1906 awarded Nobel Peace Prize for his role in ending war between Japan and Russia. In 1906 attains passage of first

	pure food law. Encourages conservation. Writes editorials and commentaries for *The Outlook* and other publications.
1912	Runs as Bullmoose Party candidate for third term as president, defeated.
1913	Publishes *An Autobiography*.
1913–1914	Exploration trip to Brazil nearly ends in his death in jungle; river named after him (Rio Teodoro); Brazil trip followed by African safari and triumphal tour of European capitals; represents the United States at funeral of Britain's King Edward VII.
1916	Declines presidential nomination of Progressive Party.
1917	Appeals to President Woodrow Wilson for a "Roosevelt Division" to fight in First World War and is turned down.
1918	Sons fight in France in World War I; the youngest, Quentin, killed in action.
1919	Dies in bed at Sagamore Hill home at Oyster Bay in New York (January 6) of arterial blood clot.

Books by Theodore Roosevelt

1881 *The Naval War of 1812*

1885 *Hunting Trips of a Ranchman*

1887 *Thomas Hart Benton*

1888 *Essays on Practical Politics*
Gouverneur Morris
Ranch Life and the Hunting Trail

1889– *The Winning of the West*
1896 (4 vols.)

1891 *New York*

1893 *The Wilderness Hunter*
American Big Game
(co-editor, contributor, with George Bird Grinnel)

1895 *Hero Tales of American History* (co-author with Henry Cabot Lodge)

1897 *American Ideals*

1899 *The Rough Riders*

1900 *Oliver Cromwell*
The Strenuous Life

1902 *The Deer Family* (co-author with T. S. van Dyke and D. G. Elliott)

1905 *Outdoor Pastimes of an American Hunter*

1907 *Good Hunting*

1909 *Outlook Editorials*

1910 *African and European Addresses*

African Game Trails
American Problems
The New Nationalism
Presidential Addresses and State Papers and European Addresses (8 vols.)

1912 *The Conservation of Womanhood and Childhood*
Realizable Ideals

1913 *An Autobiography*
History as Literature and Other Essays
Progressive Principles

1914 *Life-Histories of African Game Animals*, (co-author with Edmund Heller)
Through the Brazilian Wilderness

1915 *America and the World War*

1916 *A Book-Lover's Holidays in the Open*
Fear God and Take Your Own Part

1917 *The Foes of Our Own Household*
National Strength and International Duty

1918 *The Great Adventure*

Books about Theodore Roosevelt

Abbott, Lawrence F. *Impressions of Theodore Roosevelt*. Garden City, N.Y.:
      Doubleday, Page and Company, 1922.

Bishop, Joseph Bucklin. *Theodore Roosevelt and His Time*. New York:
      Charles Scribner's Sons, 1973.

Blum, John Morton. *The Republican Roosevelt*. Cambridge, Mass.: Harvard
      University Press, 1954.

Brands, H. W. *T R: The Last Romantic*. New York: Basic Books, 1997.

Burton, David H. *Theodore Roosevelt*. New York: Twayne Publishers, 1972.

Busch, Noel. *T. R.: The Story of Theodore Roosevelt and His Influence on Our
      Times*. New York: Reynal and Company, 1963.

Hagedorn, Hermann, ed. *The Free Citizen*. New York: Macmillan, 1956.

_____. *The Roosevelt Family of Sagamore Hill*. New York: Macmillan, 1954.

Harbaugh, William. *Power and Responsibility*. New York: Farrar, Straus and
      Cudahy, 1961.

Harlow, Alvin. *Theodore Roosevelt, Strenuous American*. New York: Julian
      Messner, 1943.

Hunt, John Gabriel, ed. *The Essential Theodore Roosevelt*. New York:
      Gramercy Books, 1994.

Jeffers, H. Paul. *Commissioner Roosevelt: The Story of Theodore Roosevelt and
      the New York City Police*. New York: John Wiley & Sons, 1994.

_____. *Colonel Roosevelt: Theodore Roosevelt Goes to War, 1897–1898*. New
      York: John Wiley & Sons, 1996.

McCullough, David. *Mornings on Horseback*. New York: Simon & Schuster,
      1981.

Miller, Nathan. *Theodore Roosevelt, a Life*. New York: William Morrow and
      Company, 1992.

Morris, Edmund. *The Rise of Theodore Roosevelt*. New York: Coward,
      McCann and Geoghegan, 1979.

Riis, Jacob. *Theodore Roosevelt, the Citizen*. New York: Outlook, 1904.

Roosevelt, Theodore. *The Rough Riders*. New York: Scribner, 1902.

_____. *An Autobiography*. New York: Macmillan, 1913.

Wister, Owen. *Roosevelt, the Story of a Friendship*. New York: Macmillan,
      1930.

Index

New York Board of Police
    Commissioners, 2, 17, 152–53,
    159
New York City, 79, 96–97
Nicholas Nickleby (Dickens), 16
Nixon, Richard M., 141
Nobel Peace Prize, 4, 97–99,
    159–60

O
Obedience, 83
Oliver Cromwell, 28, 50, 89, 159
Optimism, 99
Organized labor, 99–100
The Outlook, 160
Overcentralization, 95

P
Panama Canal, 4, 100–101
Patriotism, 101
Pershing, John J., 156
Philosophy, 101
Platt, Thomas, 154
Play, 102
Pluck, 104
Political campaign contributions,
    104
Politics, 104–6
Posterity, 106
Power, 107, 134
Preseverance, 21
Presidency, 107–9, 134. *See also*
    Government; Vice-presidency
Principles, 109

Progressive Party, 160
Public service, 110
Pure Food Law, 4, 123–24

Q
Quack remedies, 50

R
Reform, 110, 112
Religion, 113–14. *See also*
    Christianity
Riding, 114
Righteousness, 43
Riis, Jacob A., 107, 155
Rio Teodoro, 5, 160
The Rise of Theodore Roosevelt
    (Morris), 6
Robinson, Douglas, 146
Roosevelt, Alice (daughter), 158
Roosevelt, Alice Lee (first wife),
    158
Roosevelt, Anna (sister), 144
Roosevelt, Archibald (son), 158
Roosevelt, Corinne (sister), 143,
    144, 147
Roosevelt, Edith Kermit Carow
    (second wife), 5, 143, 158
Roosevelt, Ethel (daughter), 158
Roosevelt, Franklin D., 40, 108
Roosevelt, Kermit (son), 16, 22, 97,
    108, 125, 138, 158
Roosevelt, Quentin (son), 5, 64–65,
    140, 159, 160
Roosevelt, Theodore

accomplishments of, 1–3, 4
books about, 162
books by, 161
chronology, 158–60
description of, 3, 4
legacy of, 7
nicknames for, 1
quotations about, 150–57
speeches by, 3–4
use of body language by, 3–4
Roosevelt, Theodore, Jr. (Ted)
(son), 54, 67, 158
Root, Elihu, 155
Rough Riders, 2, 6, 142–49, 150,
159
The Rough Riders, 159
Rudolph, Cuno Hugo, 102
Russo-Japanese War, 68

S
Sagamore Hill, 81
San Juan Hill, 2, 6
Science, 43
Self-government, 12, 59
Self-interest, 38
Self-reliance, 21, 115
Self-respect, 111, 115, 129
Shooting, 115–16. *See also* Hunting
Simplified spelling, 116–18
Sixty, turning, 125
Spanish-American War, 2, 6,
142–49
Spelling, simplified, 116–18

Sports, 118–19. *See also* Boxing;
Football; Wrestling
Spring-Rice, Cecil, 37, 68
Square deal, 4, 14, 77, 119–20
Steffens, Lincoln, 107
Strenuous life, 2
Success, 120, 122
Superstitution, 43

T
Taft, William Howard, 4
Taxes, 122
Ten Commandments, 113
Tetons, 32
Theology, 43
Tolstoy, Leo, 15
Trevelyn, Sir George Otto, 88
True Christian, 122–23
Truthfulness, 21
Truth in labeling, 123–24
Tyranny, 130

U
U.S. Civil Service Commission, 2,
152, 158

V
Veterans, 125
Vice-presidency, 115–16. *See also*
Presidency
Vigor, 20
Virtue, 126, 128
Voting, 128

OTHER TITLES OF INTEREST

ROUGH RIDERS
Theodore Roosevelt
With additional text by Richard Bak
256 pp., b/w photos throughout
0-87833-194-8
$18.95

THE SELECTED LETTERS OF THEODORE ROOSEVELT
Edited by H. W. Brands
464 pp., 20 b/w photos and illustrations
0-8154-1126-X
$32.00 cloth

THE ALAMO
An Illustrated History
Edwin P. Hoyt
208 pp., color & b/w photos throughout
0-87833-204-9
$28.95 cloth

THE ALAMO
A Cultural History
Frank Thompson
272 pp., b/w photos throughout
0-87833-254-5
$27.95

THAT'S NOT IN MY AMERICAN HISTORY BOOK
A Compilation of Little-Known Events and Forgotten Heroes
Thomas Ayres
256 pp., b/w photos & illustrations
0-87833-185-9
$19.95 cloth

THE REVOLUTIONARY WAR QUIZ AND FACT BOOK
Jonathan Hall
272 pp., b/w illustrations throughout
0-87833-226-X
$14.95

THEY RODE FOR THE LONE STAR
The Saga of the Texas Rangers
Thomas W. Knowles
208 pp., 150 color & b/w photos
0-87833-205-7
$29.95 cloth

STONEWALL JACKSON
A Life Portrait
K. M. Kostyal
224 pp., b/w photos throughout
0-87833-220-0
$29.95 cloth

BEHIND ENEMY LINES
Civil War Spies, Raiders, and Guerillas
Wilmer L. Jones, Ph.D
344 pp., b/w photos throughout
0-87833-191-3
$26.95 cloth

Available at bookstores or call 1-800-462-6420

Taylor Trade Publishing
4720 Boston Way, Lanham, MD 20706

Cooper Square Press
200 Park Avenue South, Suite 1109, New York, New York
10003
www.coopersquarepress.com